S0-AQM-866

INTRODUCTION TO
AIRCRAFT
MAINTENANCE
STUDENT WORKBOOK
REVISED EDITION

AVOTEK
INFORMATION RESOURCES

Production Staff
Editor Ian McCloskey
Lead Illustrator Amy Siever
Designer/Production Coordinator Roberta Byerly

International Standard Book Number 0-9708109-9-7
ISBN 13: 978-0-970810-99-1
Order # T-CORE-0202

For Sale by: Avotek
A Select Aerospace Industries company

Mail to:
P.O. Box 219
Weyers Cave, Virginia 24486
USA

Ship to:
200 Packaging Drive
Weyers Cave, Virginia 24486
USA

Toll Free: 1-800-828-6835
Telephone: 1-540-234-9090

Fax: 1-540-234-9399

Revised Edition
Fourth Printing
Printed in the USA

www.avotekbooks.com

www.avotek.com

Contents

To the Student

This Student Workbook accompanies *Introduction to Aircraft Maintenance*, the first in a four book series created and published by Avotek. This workbook should be utilized as a tool for highlighting the strengths as well as pinpointing the weaknesses of the AMT student gathering the skill and knowledge necessary to build a strong foundation in the aircraft maintenance field. Specifically, it evaluates the progress made in applicable subject areas.

The foundation on which this workbook has been built assumes that the student is actively engaged in preparing for two goals: the first is to pass all required testing for the FAA Airframe and Powerplant Mechanic Certificate, and the second is to obtain the necessary skills and knowledge to function as an entry-level mechanic in the field. Both goals must be kept in mind and the material presented here has been designed to maintain that balance.

Each chapter of the text is divided into three different question formats and printed on perforated sheets for removal and presentation. They are presented as follows:

Fill in the Blank

These questions are designed to help the student understand new terminology and fundamental facts essential to the understanding of section material.

Multiple Choice

These questions offer a broader overview of the material by offering several possible answers, and allowing the student to identify the correct answer either through recognition or through the process of elimination.

Analysis

These are complex questions that require the student to access information presented in the text, analyze the data, and record a response. Successful completion of the analysis questions shows the student has a thorough understanding of the material contained in the chapter.

The answers for each set of questions are available from your course instructor. ➤

Avotek® Aircraft Maintenance Series:

Introduction to Aircraft Maintenance
Aircraft Structural Maintenance
Aircraft System Maintenance
Aircraft Powerplant Maintenance

Other Books by Avotek®:

Aircraft Turbine Engines
Aircraft Corrosion Control Guide
Aircraft Structural Technician
Aircraft Wiring & Electrical Installation
Aviation Maintenance Technician Reference Handbook
Avionics: Systems and Troubleshooting
Avotek Aeronautical Dictionary
Fundamentals of Modern Aviation
Light Sport Aircraft Inspection Procedures

1. _____ is the smallest part of any substance.

2. There are _____ natural elements.

3. The _____ of a liquid is measured with a hydrometer.

4. The float in a hydrometer is indicating 1.000. It is measuring the specific gravity of _____ .

5. In aircraft maintenance a _____ is to measure the state of charge of a lead acid battery.

6. The hydrometer reading of a charged battery is _____ .

7. Energy that can be stored is called _____ energy.

8. A body in motion is said to have _____ energy.

9. Force times displacement equals _____ .

10. _____ is defined as the rate of doing work.

11. A single pulley rope system arranged as shown will _____ the pull required to lift the load.

12. To turn two shafts in the same direction using external gears it takes a gear train with an _____ number of gears.

13. The two types of basic stress are _____ and _____.

Chapter 1: *Aviation Physics*

FILL IN THE BLANK QUESTIONS

name:

date:

14. A body in motion has a property called momentum. This is an application of _____ law of motion.

15. _____ is the rate of change in velocity.

16. All heat energy can be directly, or indirectly, traced to nuclear reactions occurring in the _____ .

17. Because of their_____ solids expand less when heated than gasses or liquids.

18. Three types of heat transfer are _____ , _____ , and _____ .

19. Because _____ are non-compressible, temperature expansion is a problem.

20. Boyle's law is normally stated "The volume of enclosed dry gas varies inversely with its _____ , provided the _____ remains constant".

21. The General gas law is a combination of _____ law and _____ law.

22. Pressure at a fluid head depends on the _____ of the fluid.

23. When an article _____ it produces waves in the air. Sound is the result of those waves of air striking the eardrum.

24. The frequency of sound is called its _____ .

25. In general the speed of sound is faster in _____ , slower in _____ , and slowest in _____ .

1. The most basic of all things in physics and the material world is:
   a. Atoms
   b. Protons
   c. Matter
   d. Neutrons

2. How many natural elements are there?
   a. 120
   b. 92
   c. 96
   d. 115

3. A hydrometer is used to measure:
   a. Total moisture in the air
   b. Depth of a body of water
   c. Amount of energy in fuel
   d. Specific gravity

4. The specific gravity of pure water is:
   a. 1,250°
   b. 1.000
   c. 2.250
   d. 1.975

5. In aircraft maintenance a hydrometer is used to measure:
   a. The state of charge of a lead acid battery
   b. The relative humidity in the ambient air
   c. The state of charge in a ni-cad battery
   d. The amount of latent heat in jet fuel

6. A hydrometer reading of a discharged battery will be:
   a. 1.150
   b. 1.200
   c. 2.400
   d. 978

7. Energy that can be stored is said to be:
   a. Latent energy
   b. Potential energy
   c. Available energy

8. A body in motion is said to have what kind of energy?
   a. Kinetic
   b. Randomized
   c. Potential
   d. Electrical

9. In the metric system the unit of work is the:
   a. Joule
   b. Newton
   c. Kilogram
   d. Watt

10. In the United States power is expressed as:
    a. Miles per hour
    b. Feet per second
    c. Horsepower
    d. Kilowatts

Chapter 1:
Aviation
Physics

MULTIPLE CHOICE QUESTIONS

name:

date:

Chapter 1:

Aviation Physics

MULTIPLE CHOICE
QUESTIONS

name:

date:

11. The pulley arrangement shown below will:
    a.   Reduce effort by 50 percent
    b.   Reduce effort by 100 percent
    c.   Increase effort by 50 percent
    d.   Change the direction of the pull

12. Which of the following is **NOT** part of a planetary gear system?
    a.   Sun gear
    b.   Bell gear
    c.   Stationary gear
    d.   Ring gear

13. Which of the following is not a stress, but the result of stress:
    a.   Torsion
    b.   Bending
    c.   Shear
    d.   Strain

14. Newton's second law of motion states that when a force acts upon a body in motion, the momentum of that body is changed. The rate of change is proportional to the:
    a.   Weight of the body
    b.   Speed of the body
    c.   Applied force
    d.   Applied mass

15. In aviation speed is measured in:
    a.   Miles per hour
    b.   Kilometers per second
    c.   Knots
    d.   Kilometers per hour

16. When heat is causes the temperature of a substance to rise it is called:
    a.   Latent heat
    b.   Applied heat
    c.   Hidden heat
    d.   Sensible heat

17. Expansion of fluids is governed by the application of:
    a.   Charles's law
    b.   Gays law
    c.   Boyle's law
    d.   Ohms law

18. There are three temperature scales. They are:
    a. Celsius, Fahrenheit, and Rankine
    b. Celsius, Fahrenheit, and absolute
    c. Fahrenheit, color, and absolute
    d. Color, centigrade, and Rankine

19. Liquids are basically non-compressible but they will:
    a. Expand more than compressed nitrogen when heated
    b. All expand at the same rate
    c. Boil at 212°F
    d. Expand at different rates when heated

20. Avogadro's law states that at the same temperature and pressure equal volumes of different gasses:
    a. Contain the same pressure
    b. Contain equal numbers of molecules
    c. Contain the original number of molecules at a higher pressure
    d. Contain an different gas from the mixing

21. Boyle's law and Charles's law have been combined into one expression and is called the:
    a. Pneumatics law
    b. Combined gas law
    c. General gas law
    d. Dual States law

22. According to Pascal's law, the pressure acting on the interior surface of an odd shaped hydraulic device will:
    a. Always be the same everywhere
    b. Vary according to the shape
    c. Vary according to the temperature
    d. Always be different at different points

23. Which of the following does **NOT** produce a harmonic wave:
    a. Pendulum on a clock
    b. Balance wheel in a watch
    c. Piston in a reciprocating engine
    d. Turbine wheel in a jet engine

24. Sound is non-linear in response pattern and is measured in bels and decibels. Which of the following is incorrect?
    a. A decibel is a constant unit
    b. A decibel varies with intensity and frequency
    c. A decibel is one tenth of a bel
    d. A decibel is the lowest lever that a change of level is perceptible

25. In air, the speed of sound varies with: (pick the incorrect one)
    a. Temperature
    b. Pressure
    c. Altitude
    d. Rate

Chapter 1:
Aviation
Physics

MULTIPLE CHOICE
QUESTIONS

name:

date:

Chapter 1:
Aviation Physics

MULTIPLE CHOICE QUESTIONS

name:

date:

1. Explain the difference between the chemical nature of matter and the physical nature of matter. What are the physical states of matter?

2. Define potential energy and kinetic energy. How do they relate to the technical definition of work?

3. Suppose a 10,000-pound aircraft is lifted 8 feet in the air in 5 minutes by one person with a hoist. How much power is developed by the person cranking the hoist? How much horsepower?

4. Describe the three types of levers and the relative position of the effort, fulcrum, and weight in each.

5. Describe the five main types of stress. What is the term for the consequence of stress?

6. Newton's three laws of motion concern objects and the forces that act on them. If an object is at rest, what must happen for it to be put in motion? If an object is in motion, what must happen to it to change the way in which it is in motion?

7. What is the difference between speed and velocity? How can velocity be charted and calculated?

8. What is the rate of acceleration of an aircraft that goes from 300 miles per hour to 350 miles per hour in 20 seconds?

9. Briefly describe the three methods of heat transfer.

10. What type of pressure does an aircraft instrument generally measure? How is it related to atmospheric pressure?

11. What will happen to a gas placed under pressure? What about a liquid placed under the same amount of pressure?

12. State Boyle's law. Name three applications of it to aviation.

13. What is the difference between the transmission of forces through solids and the transmission of forces through a liquid or gas?

14. Describe Bernouli's principle and give one system on an aircraft where it applies.

15. What is the speed of an aircraft traveling at Mach 4?

Chapter 1:
Aviation
Physics

ANALYSIS
QUESTIONS

name:

date:

Chapter 1:
Aviation Physics

ANALYSIS QUESTIONS

name:

date:

1. _____ is the science of the action of air on an object.

2. A one inch^2 column of air that extends from sea level to the top of the atmosphere weighs _____ pounds.

3. Temperature is the major factor affecting the _____ properties of fluids.

4. As altitude increases, air pressure _____ .

5. On the centigrade scale water boils at _____ and freezes at _____ .

6. Humidity is the amount of _____ in the air.

7. If the temperature drops and the absolute humidity stays the same, the relative humidity will

   .

8. Still air has only one attribute. That attribute is _____ .

9. Newton's second law says that a body in motion at a uniform speed, when acted on by an outside force, will change in _____ to the force.

10. The airflow over a wing is the same as half of a _____ .

11. As air flows along the bottom surface of a wing its air pressure remains

    _____ .

12. The reverse of acceleration is _____ .

13. A typical low speed airfoil will have its thickest point about _____ of the way back of the leading edge.

14. Normally the lift of a wing will increase with an increase in _____ .

15. The ratio of wingspan to chord is called the _____ .

16. The lift on a wing can be shown as a _____ because it has

    _____ , _____ , and

    _____ .

17. The burbling point of the air over a wing is also the _____ .

18. Because airflow tends to stick to a surface and is not perfectly smooth they result in a _____ of air.

19. The force of lift always acts _____ to the relative wind.

Chapter 2:
Principles of Aerodynamics

FILL IN THE BLANK QUESTIONS

name:

date:

20. In an aircraft trimmed for level flight, more power means _____ .

21. A spanwise flow of air that flows up around the wingtip produced drag known as a _____ .

22. An airplane in flight rotates around one or more of _____ axes.

23. Dynamic stability is described as being either _____ dynamic stability or dynamic _____ .

24. The purpose of a spoiler is to _____ drag and reduce _____ .

25. Most horizontal tail surfaces are designed to produce a _____ on the __ of the aircraft.

26. The application of slats, slots, leading edge flaps, trailing edge flaps, and other such devices is known as _____ control.

27. On a standard day the speed of sound is _____ .

28. The flow right behind a normal shock wave is always _____ .

29. When reductions in airflow take place, there is a corresponding _____ in air temperature.

30. A vortex generator is a pair of small, low aspect-ratio airfoils mounted at _____ to each other.

31. Once the airflow is supersonic the aerodynamic center of the surface is located at approximately _____ .

1. Which of the following is not a distinct part of aerodynamics:
   a. The atmosphere
   b. The relative humidity
   c. The relative wind

2. As altitude increases from sea level to the top of the atmosphere, there is a predictable temperature change. This change is called a:
   a. Density altitude
   b. Barometric change
   c. Lapse rate

3. Of the four temperature scales, which one is used the least?
   a. Celsius
   b. Fahrenheit
   c. Kelvin
   d. Rankine

4. What is the barometric pressure in inches of mercury on a sea level standard day?
   a. 28.79
   b. 29.28
   c. 47.51
   d. 29.92

5. Absolute zero is a temperature reference where all molecular action ceases. It can be expressed as:
   a. 0°K
   b. -273°C
   c. -460°F
   d. All of the above

6. Which of the following statements is true?
   a. Dry air has no density and weighs nothing
   b. Water vapor weighs 5/8 as much as dry air
   c. Dry air weighs 5/8 as much as water vapor

7. When air holds water vapor, it:
   a. Is lighter than dry air
   b. Is heavier that dry air
   c. Weighs the same as dry air

8. Relative wind is caused by the:
   a. Motion of the aircraft through still air
   b. Motion of the air around a still aircraft
   c. Both

9. Newton's third law, for every action there is an equal and opposite reaction, is best demonstrated by:
   a. Magnetic attraction
   b. Gravity
   c. A rowboat

10. When air flows over the camber of a wing, the air pressure:
    a. Increases
    b. Stays the same
    c. Decreases

11. An airfoil will maintain lift any time it has air moving across it, but:
    a. In an upward direction only
    b. In any direction
    c. Only if facing into the wind.

Chapter 2:

Principles of Aerodynamics

MULTIPLE CHOICE
QUESTIONS

name:

date:

Chapter 2:
Principles of Aerodynamics

MULTIPLE CHOICE
QUESTIONS

name:

date:

12. Which of the following adds the least lift to a wing:
    a.   The airfoil shape
    b.   Downwash
    c.   Air density

13. When the angle of attack of an airfoil is increased so it reaches maximum lift, the:
    a.   Airplane can go no faster
    b.   Angle of incidence is its highest
    c.   Lift-over-drag ratio is at its highest

14. Increasing upper camber and adding lower camber and wing area is the description of a:
    a.   Split wing flap
    b.   Plain wing flap
    c.   Fowler wing flap

15. The angle of incidence is:
    a.   Adjustable for nose heaviness
    b.   Usually fixed and non-adjustable
    c.   Infinitely adjustable

16. When each small part of lift on a wing is added together mathematically the sum is called the:
    a.   Aerodynamic center
    b.   Resultant force
    c.   Aerodynamic pressure

17. The center of pressure can move fore and aft, depending on the:
    a.   Angle of incidence
    b.   Curvature of the airfoil
    c.   Angle of attack

18. When the boundary layer "breaks away" from the wing:
    a.   The wing will stall
    b.   Will generate more drag
    c.   The airflow will speed up

19. When the lift force is in equilibrium with the weight force, the aircraft will:
    a.   Dive
    b.   Climb
    c.   Fly level

20. The speed of an aircraft is controlled by its:
    a.   Pitch
    b.   Power setting
    c.   Throttle

21. A similar flow of air from the upper wing surface flows inboard towards the fuselage and produces an inner vortex. This vortex causes:
    a.   Air along the fuselage to move faster
    b.   More available air in the center of the downwash
    c.   Increased drag

22. Which of the controls match the following actions? Roll, pitch, yaw:
    a.   Ailerons, elevators, rudder
    b.   Rudder, elevators, elevator
    c.   Elevators , ailerons, rudder

23. On high speed and transport airplanes spoilers are used in place of ailerons during flight. This:
    a.   Reduces pilot effort
    b.   Reduces power requirements
    c.   Reduces wing twist

24. Spoilers are also used as speed brakes by:
    a. Reducing wing area
    b. Increasing lift
    c. Increasing drag

25. Pulling back on the yoke raises the elevator and:
    a. Increases lift
    b. Decreases lift
    c. Creates a stall

26. To keep a flat wing from stalling all at one time:
    a. A stall strip is installed.
    b. The ailerons are drooped.
    c. The aft yoke stop is adjusted.

27. A compression wave is more commonly known as:
    a. A shock wave
    b. A control reversal
    c. Subsonic pressure

28. The transition flow from supersonic to subsonic without a direction change:
    a. Always forms a normal shock wave
    b. Always increases the pressure
    c. Always happens when the air is turning a corner

29. The effects of higher temperatures due to high speed airflow:
    a. Reduces airspeed
    b. Increases fuel flow
    c. Lowers structural strength

30. One purpose of a vortex generator is to:
    a. Delay drag divergence
    b. Increase separation
    c. Create a normal shock wave

31. Aerodynamic heating of the air raises the engine inlet temperature. The increased temperature:
    a. Produces more thrust by allowing more fuel to be vaporized
    b. Reduces range by increasing fuel flow
    c. Lowers thrust by requiring lower engine internal temperatures be maintained

Chapter 2:

Principles of Aerodynamics

MULTIPLE CHOICE
QUESTIONS

name:

date:

Chapter 2:
Principles of Aerodynamics

MULTIPLE CHOICE
QUESTIONS

name:

date:

1. What happens to the density of air at higher elevations? What happens to the density of air at lower temperatures?

2. What is the definition of a standard day? How is it used in aviation?

3. What four forces act on an aircraft in flight?

4. Describe aircraft lift in terms of Bernouli's principle. What portion of aircraft lift is the result of the difference in pressure between the upper and lower surface of an airfoil?

5. Define aspect ratio. What happens to lift when aspect ratio is increased?

6. Describe how the angle of attack of a wing helps cause lift. Why does an angle of attack that is too great cause lift to drop?

7. How do you increase the speed of an aircraft? How do you increase the altitude?

8. On what three axes does an aircraft turn? What is motion around each axis called, and how is it controlled?

9. Name five types of tabs. What is the purpose of each type?

10. What is the most commonly used high-lift device? What is the purpose of a high-lift device?

11. What is the boundary layer of air over a control surface? How can it be controlled?

12. Why are winglets helpful in increasing lift?

13. What happens to air density and air velocity in an expanding tube in subsonic flight and in supersonic flight?

14. What is the angle of a normal shock wave to an object in a supersonic airflow? What is the airspeed aft of the wave relative to the speed of sound? If the airspeed in front of the normal shock wave is increased, what happens to the airspeed aft of the wave?

15. What happens to the static pressure, temperature, and density of an airstream passing through an oblique shock wave? What effect does it have on the available energy of the airstream?

Chapter 2:
Principles of
Aerodynamics

ANALYSIS
QUESTIONS

name:

date:

Chapter 2:
Principles of Aerodynamics

ANALYSIS QUESTIONS

name:

date:

1. _____ is a numbering system that only uses two numbers—zero and one.

2. The numbering system used in most everyday counting and math is called the _____ .

3. _____ is the process of combining two or more numbers in order to determine the total.

4. Subtraction is the process of finding the _____ between two numbers.

5. _____ is the process of finding out how many times one number is contained in another number.

6. _____ is the process of adding a number to itself a given number of times.

7. The decimal fraction 6.07 can be read as six and _____ .

8. When adding a series of decimal fractions, first align the _____ vertically.

9. In a fraction, the number below the line is known as the _____ .

10. _____ represents numbers in term of powers of ten.

11. The expression 10^6 is the more commonly stated as _____ .

12. A fraction where the numerator is greater than the denominator can also be expressed as a ___ .

13. If 3/9 is written as _____ , we say that the fraction has been reduced to its lowest terms.

14. To multiply one fraction by another, multiply the _____ , then multiply the _____ .

15. To divide one fraction by another, invert the _____ and multiply the two fractions.

16. The decimal number _____ can also be expressed as 12%.

17. A ratio can be expressed three ways: as a _____ , using a colon, or as a decimal number.

Chapter 3:
General
Mathematics

FILL IN THE BLANK QUESTIONS

name:

date:

Chapter 3:
General Mathematics

FILL IN THE BLANK QUESTIONS

name:

date:

18. The _____ of a cylinder is the ratio of the cylinder's volume when the piston is at bottom center, to the cylinder's volume when the piston is at top center.

19. A proportion is a statement of _____ between two or more ratios.

20. In the expression 5^2, or "five squared," 5 is the base and 2 is the _____ .

21. _____ is expressed as square units, such as square feet or square centimeters.

22. To find the area of a rectangle or parallelogram, multiple the _____ by the width.

23. The area of a triangle is equal to one half the product of the base and the _____ .

24. The shape pictured below is called a _____ .

25. $A=1/2(b_1+b_2)h$ is the formula used to determine the area of a _____ . In the formula, h represents the _____ of the shape.

26. In most cases, 3.1416 is sufficiently accurate to substitute for the number _____ .

27. In the picture below, the line labeled "A" is called the _____ and the line labeled "B" is called the _____ .

28. The formula for the area of a _____ is $A = \varpi r^2$.

29. When one wants to determine how much liquid a tank can hold, one must determine the _____ of the tank.

30. To find the volume of a rectangular solid, multiply the _____ by the __ by the _____ .

31. The formula for the volume of a cylinder is _____ .

32. The volume of a sphere is determined by multiplying the _____ of the diameter by one-sixth of ϖ, or 0.5236.

33. _____ deals with relationships between the lengths of the three sides and three angles of a triangle.

34. In the picture below, the line labeled "C" is called the _____ .

35. A _____ is a chart showing solutions to formulas involving several mathematical operations.

36. The standard English unit of length is the foot; the standard unit of length in the International Metric System is the _____ .

37. The basic unit of _____ in both the English and International Metric systems is the second.

38. The standard unit of mass in the English system is the ounce. In the International Metric System, the standard unit of mass is the _____ .

39. If you know the diameter of a wheel in centimeters, you can determine the diameter in inches by multiplying the centimeters by _____ .

40. To convert gallons to _____ , multiply by 3.8.

41. One square _____ equals 6.5 square centimeters.

42. The _____ is a unit of force in the International Metric System.

43. The metric prefix "kilo" means one thousand. Thus, a kilometer equals _____ meters.

44. The square root of 86 is _____ .

45. The square of 86 is _____ .

FILL IN THE BLANK QUESTIONS

name:

date:

Chapter 3:
General Mathematics

FILL IN THE BLANK QUESTIONS

name:

date:

1. What is the decimal number equivalent of the binary number 10?
   a. 20
   b. 2
   c. 3
   d. 27^{-10}

2. The decimal number 5.003 is read as:
   a. Five and three tenths
   b. Five and three hundredths
   c. Five and three thousandths
   d. Three and three hundredths

3. What is the total resistance of a circuit where the individual resistors are 3.21 ohms, 29.1 ohms, and 0.07 ohms?
   a. 32.38 ohms
   b. 33.01 ohms
   c. 11.682 ohms
   d. 12.1 ohms

4. What is the remainder when 0.003 is subtracted from 0.1?
   a. 0.97
   b. 0.970
   c. 0.0003
   d. 0.097

5. What is the product of 0.1 and 0.003?
   a. 0.03
   b. 0.103
   c. 0.0003
   d. 0.00003

6. The number 10,000 is represented in scientific notation as:
   a. 1^{0000}
   b. 1^{10}
   c. 10^4
   d. 10^5

7. The expression "5 to the fourth power" is written as:
   a. 4^5
   b. 5^4
   c. 5^{-4}
   d. 4^{-5}

8. In a fraction, the number above the line is called the:
   a. Subdenominator
   b. Denominator
   c. Supernumerary
   d. Numerator

9. The sum of 3/4 and 5/16, stated in its lowest terms, is:
   a. 14/16
   b. 15/64
   c. 7/8
   d. 17/16

10. The sum of 5/8 and 13/16, expressed as a mixed number, is:
    a. 1-1/8
    b. 23/16
    c. 18/16
    d. 1-7/16

Chapter 3:
General
Mathematics

MULTIPLE CHOICE
QUESTIONS

name:

date:

Chapter 3:
General Mathematics

MULTIPLE CHOICE
QUESTIONS

name:

date:

11. The fraction 25/80, stated in its lowest terms, is:
    a. 1/8
    b. 5/16
    c. 3/8
    d. 20/75

12. The product of 5/8 and 3/4, reduced to its lowest terms, is:
    a. 15/32
    b. 5/12
    c. 11/8
    d. 1/2

13. If 21.67722 were rounded to the nearest hundredth, the result would be:
    a. 21.7
    b. 21
    c. 21.68
    d. 21.67

14. The sum of 5 and –3 is:
    a. 2
    b. 8
    c. 15
    d. –2

15. The product of two negative numbers is always:
    a. Zero
    b. Positive
    c. Negative
    d. Unknowable

16. The aspect ratio of an aircraft is a comparison of the wing span to the:
    a. Fuel capacity
    b. Wing nut
    c. Wing chord
    d. Cylinder volume when the piston is at the bottom of the cylinder

17. If an airplane uses 40 gallons of fuel to fly 400 miles, how many gallons will it require to fly 600 miles?
    a. 100
    b. 60
    c. 45
    d. 50

18. The area of a square whose sides are 4 inches long is:
    a. 8 in²
    b. 12 in²
    c. 16 in²
    d. 4 in²

19. The area of a rectangle 3 feet long and 6 feet wide is:
    a. 9 ft²
    b. 18 ft²
    c. 20 ft²
    d. 15 ft²

20. The area of a rectangle 3 feet long and 6 feet wide is
    a. 1 yd²
    b. 1.5 yd²
    c. 18 yd²
    d. 2 yd²

21. The area of the triangle shown at right is:
    a. 6 cm²
    b. 12 cm²
    c. 20 cm²
    d. 43 cm²

MULTIPLE CHOICE
QUESTIONS

name:

22. The area of the parallelogram shown at right is:
    a. 10 in
    b. 7 in²
    c. 10 in²
    d. 5 in²

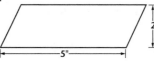

date:

23. The area of the trapezoid shown at right is:
    a. 11 m²
    b. 9 m²
    c. 18 m²
    d. 36 m²

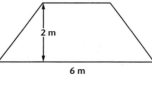

24. The area of the circle shown at right is:
    a. π8²
    b. π8
    c. π4²
    d. π16²

25. The volume of a cube measuring 3 inches on each side is:
    a. 30 in³
    b. 9 in²
    c. 27 in²
    d. 27 in³

26. A rectangular solid measures 2 yards by 4 yards by 5 yards. Its volume is:
    a. 40 yd³
    b. 15 yd³
    c. 11 yd³
    d. 28 yd³

27. The volume of the solid in Question 26, converted to cubic feet, is:
    a. 3 ft³
    b. 33 ft³
    c. 270 ft³
    d. 1080 ft³

28. A cylinder has a radius of 4 cm and a height of 5 cm. What is its volume?
    a. π(4²)(5) cm³
    b. π(4²)(5²) cm³
    c. π(4)(5) cm³
    d. π(2)(5) cm³

29. A sphere has a diameter of 20 inches. What is its volume?
    a. (π/6)(20) in³
    b. (π/6)(20²) in³
    c. (π/6)(10³) in³
    d. (π/6)(20³) in³

30. One cubic meter equals how many cubic centimeters?
    a. 10³
    b. 100³
    c. 300
    d. 1,000

Chapter 3:
General Mathematics

MULTIPLE CHOICE QUESTIONS

name:

date:

31. According to Table 3-21-1, what is the sine of a 33-degree angle?
    a. 42
    b. .5299
    c. .5592
    d. .5446

32. According to Figure 3-22-2, what percent of sea level power is available at an altitude of 6,000 feet?
    a. More than you will ever need
    b. 75 percent
    c. 60 percent
    d. 80 percent

33. Which system of measurement is used most frequently throughout the world?
    a. English
    b. French
    c. Metric
    d. Canadian

34. How is speed quantified in the International Metric System?
    a. Weeks per month
    b. Miles per hour
    c. Meters per second
    d. Newtons per meter

35. How long, in yards, is a 3,000-meter runway?
    a. 3,100
    b. 1.1
    c. 3,000
    d. 3,300

36. How many grams does a 6-ounce object weigh?
    a. 168
    b. 186
    c. 2.37
    d. 1,680

37. What International Metric System prefix means "one billion times"?
    a. Tera
    b. Giga
    c. Mega
    d. Micro

38. What is the decimal equivalent of 43/64?
    a. 5/8
    b. 0.7232
    c. 17.07
    d. 0.6720

39. What is the cube of 3?
    a. 9
    b. 27
    c. 12
    d. 3

40. What is the square root of 59?
    a. 3,481
    b. 205,379
    c. 7.6811
    d. 3.8930

1. A circuit's total resistance is 30.02 ohms. There are three resistors. You know that one of them has a resistance of 25.66 ohms, and that another one has a resistance of 2.97 ohms. What is the resistance of the third resistor?

2. The wing area of an airplane is equal to the product of the wing span and the wing chord. The wing area of an airplane is 300 square feet. The wing span is 56 feet. What is the chord of the wing, to the nearest hundredth of a foot?

3. Using the final answer to Question 2, express the airplane's wing chord in feet and inches. Round to the nearest inch.

4. Convert your answer to Question 3 to centimeters.

5. The aspect ratio of an aircraft compares the wing span to the wing chord. On a certain airplane, the wing span is 45 feet and the wing chord is 6 feet. Express this ratio in three different ways. Reduce to lowest terms, where applicable.

6. Under normal operating conditions, an airplane can fly 200 miles on 21 gallons of fuel. If the pilot plans to fly 550 miles, how many gallons of fuel will be needed? Round your answer to the nearest tenth of a gallon.

7. A hangar has a floor area of 15,028 square feet. You need to measure the space to determine how many aircraft can fit in it. It is Friday, and you are tired, so you measure only the short side of the rectangular hangar; it is 68 feet long. If the airplanes in question are 51 feet long, how many will fit, end to end, along the longer side of the hangar?

8. You need to determine the length of one side of a trapezoid. You know that the total area of the polygon is 300 m². You also know that the longer base measures 30 meters, and that the shape is 12 meters high. How long is the second base?

9. An airplane taxiing on a runway has a turning radius of 30 feet. How wide must the runway be to allow the airplane to complete a 180-degree turn?

10. If the airplane in Question 8 made a complete, 360-degree turn, what would be the area of the circle outlined by its front wheel? Round your answer to the nearest hundredth of a foot.

11. You need to move a number of barrels from a storage area to a hangar. You read on the side of the barrel that each contains 17.18 cubic feet of material. Each barrel comes up to your waist, which you know to be 3-1/2 feet high. If the cart on which you will transport the barrels is 10 feet long and 3 feet wide, how many barrels can you fit on the cart at one time?

Chapter 3: *General Mathematics*

ANALYSIS QUESTIONS

name:

date:

Chapter 3:
General
Mathematics

ANALYSIS
QUESTIONS

name:

date:

12. A liquid oxygen converter comes in boxes that measure 15 centimeters on each side. If you stacked the boxes in a cube, three boxes wide, three boxes deep, and three boxes high, what volume of shelf space would the boxes occupy?

13. Assume that the liquid oxygen converters in the boxes described are spherical and that they touch the sides of the box that contains them. (Also assume that the inside of the box measures 15 cm.) What is the volume of one of the liquid oxygen converters to the nearest cubic centimeter? What percentage (to the nearest whole number) of the volume of the box does the sphere fill?

14. The stroke of a cylinder is 5 inches. The cylinder has a bore of 4-1/5 inches. What is the piston displacement of the cylinder? If the engine has six cylinders, what is the total displacement? Round the answers to the nearest one-fourth of a cubic inch and express them as mixed numbers in their lowest terms.

15. A cylinder has a bore of 12 centimeters. The height of the cylinder when the piston is at top center is 1 centimeter. The height of the cylinder when the piston is at bottom center is 8 centimeters. What is the compression ratio of the cylinder? Calculate volumes to the nearest cubic centimeter. Express the ratio in three ways (one of them to the nearest hundredth).

1. Wash grease and dirt from tools with _____ .

2. When using compressed air do not exceed _____ p.s.i.g.

3. Tools left in the wrong places can cause damage to equipment, referred to as

    _____ .

4. All machinery in the shop that can move due to vibration should be

    _____ .

5. _____ means all tools are where they belong at all times.

6. A tool that can prove the surface is a true vertical is a _____ .

7. _____ can start if a scribed line is left on the material.

8. The _____ is a tool used to measure distances beyond the range of calipers.

9. Digital instruments are _____ , meaning the accuracy is self-adjusted
    each time they are turned on.

10. In the most commonly used micrometers, the range is _____ .

11. A _____ micrometer is used to measure recesses or holes.

12. A _____ depth gauge can enter a 1/32 inch slot, but not a hole less
    than 1/4 inch in diameter.

13. A _____ depth gauge can enter a 3/32 inch hole but not a 1/32 inch slot.

14. A NO GO ring gauge is smaller than the GO ring gauge and further distinguished by a/an
    _____ in the knurled outer surface.

15. GO gauges measure the _____ of fit of mating parts, while NO GO
    gauges measure the _____ of fit.

16. Always use eye protection when using _____ hammers.

17. A _____ cross-point screwdriver has a sharp point, while a
    _____ has a blunt tip and they are not interchangeable.

18. Electric screwdrivers should not be used around _____ as they can be
    an explosion hazard.

19. _____ wrenches are used to tighten or remove screws with hexagonal
    recesses.

Chapter 4:
*Tools and
Techniques*

**FILL IN THE BLANK
QUESTIONS**

name:

date:

Chapter 4: *Tools and Techniques*

FILL IN THE BLANK QUESTIONS

name:

date:

20. A _____ wrench is used when a bolt is in a location where an obstruction prevents the use of a socket or a full size wrench.

21. _____ wrenches should be used only when wrenches of the correct size are unavailable.

22. _____ wrenches are used on special nuts with holes or notches found in propeller systems.

23. Pliers should never be used as a substitute for a _____ .

24. To prevent scratching and denting of soft substances when clamping, install _____ on the vise jaws.

25. When glass or highly polished objects are clamped, use _____ or _____ to protect them from localized stress and damage.

26. When grinding a chisel, if the edge _____ you have destroyed the temper and the chisel will not hold an edge.

27. Hollow punches are also called _____ .

28. When laying out work to be drilled, place a _____ behind the metal to prevent denting.

29. The amount of pressure to be applied while drilling depends on the _____ and the _____ .

30. Never turn a reamer _____ .

31. Turning a reamer too slowly or too quickly will cause it to _____ , producing _____ hole.

32. Never use a sulphur-based cutting oil on _____ as the sulphur can be absorbed into the pores of the metal and cause _____ .

33. When a broken tap does not protrude, it should be completely removed with a/an _____ .

34. _____ are used to cut inside, or female, threads and _____ are used for cutting outside, or male, threads.

35. You would use a _____ to tighten a B nut on a pneumatic tube.

36. After using an audible-click torque wrench, _____ .

37. Before using a torque wrench, check it for _____ .

38. When grinding soft materials or to remove a large amount of material, a _____ grinding wheel should be used.

39. The single most important safety precaution when using power tools is _____ .

40. Shrinking, stretching and planishing hammers are _____ hammers.

41. Use a _____ to remove the valve stem from a tire when replacing a wheel assembly.

42. A cable tensiometer's _____ lets you take cable tension measurements when the dial is difficult to see.

43. If you drop a torque wrench on the floor, _____ before further use.

44. Flexible beam torque wrenches have _____ to maintain proper distance from the socket drive and ensure an accurate reading.

45. Before using a spiral screw extractor you must _____ .

46. _____ are used to cut threads when an extremely tight fit is necessary.

47. When using a reamer on steel, you should _____ .

48. You should never use a reamer to remove more than _____ of metal.

49. A _____ is used to ream holes for taper pins.

50. _____ in a drill allow chips to escape and let lubricate reach the drill's cutting edges.

51. _____ diestocks are usually used with rectangular pipe dies.

52. The two main types of cleaning guns are the _____ and the _____ .

53. When using air drill motors always remove the _____ immediately after it is used or it will fly loose when the drill is started.

54. Air-powered wrenches of any type are not normally used in aircraft maintenance because of the difficulty in _____ .

Chapter 4:
Tools and Techniques

FILL IN THE BLANK QUESTIONS

name:

date:

Chapter 4:
Tools and Techniques

FILL IN THE BLANK QUESTIONS

name:

date:

55. Use a _____ to drill holes when you do not have access to electric or pneumatic power.

56. To avoid injury, never use a file that lacks _____ .

57. A grinding wheel has a wheel on each end of the motor shaft, one of which is used for _____ work and one of which is used for _____ purposes.

58. Grinding wheels should not be used to grind _____ .

59. The _____ of a drill bit do the actual cutting.

60. Alternating the angle of the file as it is drawn across the work is called _____ .

61. The accuracy of most torque wrenches decreases _____ .

62. A propeller protractor's indicating edge is opposite its _____ .

63. A _____ is very useful when you have to torque a large number of screws, as when you are installing a large floor panel.

64. An outside micrometer should be periodically checked for _____ .

65. When using a sheet metal and wire gauge, the measurement is taken _____ .

Chapter 4:
Tools and
Techniques

MULTIPLE CHOICE
QUESTIONS

name:

date:

1. Flammable materials should be stored in/on:
   a. The shop floor
   b. An open bin and uncovered to allow for fumes to escape
   c. An OSHA-approved area
   d. A tool box

2. Plumb bobs are most useful in establishing measurement:
   a. During weight and balance checks
   b. For horizontal surface reference points
   c. In surveying
   d. With a chalk line

3. Which of these is used to determine the center of cylindrical work?
   a. Bevel protractor square
   b. Rule with a center head
   c. Carpenter's square
   d. Protractor

4. Which of these has an acute angle attachment for measuring acute angles accurately?
   a. Bevel protractor square
   b. Rule with a center head
   c. Carpenter's square
   d. Protractor

5. Which of these is **NOT** to be used on a metal surface as it could lead to galvanic corrosion?
   a. Graphite pencil
   b. Marking pencil
   c. Scriber
   d. Setscrew

6. The vernier caliper can measure a distance as small as:
   a. 1/10th of an inch
   b. 1/100th of an inch
   c. 1/1000th of an inch
   d. 1/10,000th of an inch

7. The most accurate adjustable measuring instrument is the:
   a. Digital caliper
   b. Micrometer
   c. Vernier caliper
   d. Trammel

8. One complete and exact revolution of the micrometer thimble moves the spindle toward or away from the anvil exactly:
   a. 0.0025 inch
   b. 0.25 inch
   c. 0.40 inch
   d. 0.025 inch

9. The vernier micrometer can measure a distance as small as:
   a. 1/10th of an inch
   b. 1/100th of an inch
   c. 1/1000th of an inch
   d. 1/10,000th of an inch

10. Which of these gauges helps to select the correct sizes of nuts, bolts and screws?
    a. Height gauge
    b. Depth gauge
    c. Thread gauge
    d. Surface gauge

Chapter 4:

Tools and Techniques

MULTIPLE CHOICE
QUESTIONS

name:

date:

11. For precise measurement of thread pitch on threaded fasteners, use a:
    a. Plug gauge
    b. Thread gauge
    c. Height gauge
    d. Depth gauge

12. Which class of ring gauge tolerance is manufactured to the highest accuracy limit?
    a. Class ZZ
    b. Class Y
    c. Class X
    d. Class Z

13. Which of these gauges helps in deciding if a part is worn beyond an allowable tolerance?
    a. Thickness gauge
    b. Dial indicator
    c. Radius gauge
    d. Fillet gauge

14. Which type of hammer is used to avoid creating sparks?
    a. Lead or copper hammer
    b. Ball peen hammer
    c. Body hammer
    d. Soft-faced hammer

15. With which type of screwdriver must you maintain constant pressure and keep the blade from slipping out of the screw head slot to avoid damage to the surrounding structure?
    a. Offset
    b. Ratchet
    c. Cross-point
    d. Phillips

16. Which type of wrench should be used whenever possible since it provides the best protection to both the user and the equipment?
    a. Box-end
    b. Open-end
    c. Adjustable
    d. Pipe

17. Which type of socket wrench handle is used when additional leverage or torque is needed to loosen nuts or bolts?
    a. Ratchet
    b. Sliding T-bar
    c. Hinged
    d. Adjustable

18. Which type of socket wrench handle is best when working around other objects?
    a. Ratchet
    b. Sliding T-bar
    c. Hinged
    d. Adjustable

19. Which of these types of wrenches is most likely to round off the corners of the nut?
    a. Open-end
    b. Box-end
    c. Socket
    d. Allen

20. Where practical, which type of wrench is best for loosening or tightening nuts and bolts?
    a. Open-end
    b. Box-end
    c. Socket
    d. Adjustable

21. Which type of pliers should **NOT** be used to hold or grip objects?
    a. Long-nose
    b. Slip-joint
    c. Vise-grip
    d. Diagonal-cutting

22. Which type of pliers should **NOT** be used to loosen or tighten cannon plugs and other electrical plugs as they will damage the connector?
    a. Water pump
    b. Slip-joint
    c. Long-nose
    d. Retaining ring

23. Which type of pliers should **NOT** be used on nuts, bolts, tube fittings or other objects which must be reused?
    a. Flat-nose
    b. Long-nose
    c. Vise-grip
    d. Slip-joint

24. Which type of chisel is used to cut square corners?
    a. Cape
    b. Diamond-point
    c. Flat
    d. Cold

25. To prevent injury while grinding a chisel, always wear:
    a. An apron
    b. Gloves
    c. Eye protection
    d. Hard hat

26. When grinding a chisel, preserve the temper by:
    a. Dipping frequently in water
    b. Grind one side at a time
    c. Grease it before grinding
    d. Keep the cutting edge straight

27. A drive punch is also called a:
    a. Drift punch
    b. Prick punch
    c. Taper punch
    d. Transfer punch

28. To prevent overheating of the teeth, strokes with a file should not exceed:
    a. 40 per minute
    b. 60 per minute
    c. 30 per minute
    d. 80 per minute

29. What do you use to clean a file?
    a. File brush
    b. File card
    c. Magnet
    d. Abrasive cloth

30. When an item needs a hole of an exact size, it must be:
    a. Drilled
    b. Reamed
    c. Automatic center punched
    d. Drive punched

Chapter 4:
Tools and Techniques

MULTIPLE CHOICE QUESTIONS

name:

date:

Chapter 4:
Tools and Techniques

31. The type of tap to use to start a thread is a:
    a. Taper
    b. Pipe
    c. Bottoming
    d. Plug

32. The type of tap to use when an extremely tight fit is necessary is a:
    a. Taper
    b. Pipe
    c. Bottoming
    d. Plug

33. The type of dies used for restoring damaged or rusty thread on screws or bolts are:
    a. Solid dies
    b. Pipe dies
    c. Open-adjusting type
    d. Screw-adjusting type

34. To measure the diameter of a hole smaller than 1/2 inch, you should use:
    a. A telescoping gauge
    b. A small hole gauge
    c. A dial caliper
    d. A wire gauge

35. To measure the diameter of a cylinder bore you would use:
    a. A telescoping gauge
    b. A dial caliper
    c. A vernier caliper
    d. An outside divider

36. When using an audible-click torque wrench, apply torque until the wrench:
    a. Smokes
    b. Slips
    c. Turns
    d. Clicks

37. When measuring a clearance with a feeler gauge, if a leaf of the proper thickness is not available you should:
    a. Give up
    b. Use two leaves that add up to the dimension you need
    c. Use a dial caliper
    d. Use a wire gauge

38. Cable tensiometers:
    a. Are direct reading
    b. Measure cable tension in psi
    c. Need a chart to convert the meter reading into the actual cable tension reading
    d. Compensate for temperature

39. Hammers that have replaceable faces and are frequently used on machined or polished surfaces are called:
    a. Copper hammers
    b. Soft-faced hammers
    c. Rawhide mallets
    d. Body hammers

40. What is used to remove broken screws without damaging the surrounding metal or threaded hole?
    a. Flat chisel
    b. Drive punch
    c. Screw extractor
    d. Electric screwdriver in reverse

41. Before connecting an air hose for use with a pneumatic tool to an air outlet, open the shutoff valve momentarily to expel:
    a. Condensation
    b. Built-up compressed air
    c. Dirt
    d. None of the above

42. When changing grinding stones for a pneumatic grinder, always make sure the replacement stone is of the correct rated:
    a. Density
    b. Speed
    c. Shape
    d. Color

43. A pneumatic tool you could use to cut panels or metal sheet is called a:
    a. Die grinder
    b. Ketts panel saw
    c. A hacksaw
    d. A pneumatic grinder

44. When using a hollow punch to cut holes in leather or rubber gasket, protect the tool by using:
    a. A rubber mallet
    b. A lead or copper mallet
    c. A wood handle
    d. A plywood or masonite backup material

45. Failing to clean a file results in:
    a. Damage to the file
    b. Rough cuts on the filed surface
    c. Marks on the filed surface
    d. All of the above

46. When cutting a rectangular hole in an instrument panel to install a new instrument, you would form precise corners by using:
    a. Radius gauges
    b. A large drill bit
    c. A round file
    d. Both A and C

47. The ground pin on an electric tool power cord reduces the possibility of:
    a. Electric shock
    b. The tool failing
    c. Incorrect voltage in the power source
    d. The cord being too short

48. One common manufactured abrasive with which a grinding wheel is composed is:
    a. Emery
    b. Diamond
    c. Silicon carbide
    d. Magnesium

49. Crossfiling is done to produce:
    a. An exceptionally flat surface
    b. An angled surface
    c. A channel or groove in the material
    d. A right-angled finish

50. When twisting safety wire with lockwire pliers, you should:
    a. Twist the safety wire as tightly as possible
    b. Avoid overstressing or damaging the safety wire
    c. Untwist the safety wire to get the required length
    d. Hold the handles tightly as you twist the wire

Chapter 4:
Tools and Techniques

MULTIPLE CHOICE QUESTIONS

name:

date:

Chapter 4:

Tools and Techniques

MULTIPLE CHOICE
QUESTIONS

name:

date:

51. When preparing a piece of metal for drilling, a shallow center punch depth:
    a. Will cause the drill bit to bind
    b. Is preferred, since it minimizes damage to the metal
    c. Helps the drill bit start in the metal
    d. Will allow the drill bit to slip out and wander

52. When using an adjustable wrench:
    a. The force on the nut should be applied by the stationary jaw of the wrench.
    b. The force on the nut should be applied by the moveable jaw of the wrench.
    c. It doesn't matter how you use an adjustable wrench.
    d. Adjustable wrenches are not allowed for aircraft use.

53. When clamping an assembly in a bench vise you should:
    a. Tighten the jaws as hard as you can.
    b. Unlock the swivel base for ease of access.
    c. Use soft metal caps on the jaws to protect the assembly's surfaces.
    d. Ensure the jaws of the vise are rough to prevent work slippage.

54. You should use Vise-grip pliers:
    a. Whenever you have the opportunity
    b. As a last resort on parts that you will not reuse
    c. In any application where you would use a wrench
    d. Vise-grips are not allowed on aircraft applications

55. Which hammer is most often used for general applications?
    a. Ball peen hammer
    b. Rubber mallet
    c. Claw hammer
    d. Body hammer

56. After cutting internal threads on a critical component, you would check the threads with:
    a. A GO plug gauge
    b. A thread gauge
    c. A NO GO plug gauge
    d. Both A and C

57. What advantage does a dial vernier caliper have over a digital caliper?
    a. They are more accurate
    b. They are self-adjusting
    c. They are more expensive
    d. They don't need batteries

58. After taking a measurement with an inside micrometer, it is a good idea to:
    a. Lubricate it thoroughly and return it to its box.
    b. Check the measurement with a micrometer caliper.
    c. Return it to zero.
    d. Clean the contact points.

59. A cable tensiometer can give an incorrect reading:
    a. If it lacks a pointer lock
    b. If a temperature compensation chart is used
    c. If the incorrect risers are used
    d. When you convert the dial reading to pounds on the chart

60. The side of a grinding wheel:
    a. Generally should not be used for grinding
    b. Is commonly used for sharpening the lips on worn drill bits
    c. Can put a fine edge on a chisel
    d. Causes no harm to the grinding wheel

1. You are working a C check on a Boeing 737, which is in a hangar with fairings and access panels removed. You are assigned a sheet metal repair that requires you to replace nutplates on a wingtip. What kind of drill motor would you **NOT** use, and why?

2. What precautions would you take when using pneumatic tools?

3. You are applying final torque to the cylinder retaining nuts on a reciprocating engine. The engine is on the wing, and your access to the nuts is limited. Discuss the tools and techniques you would use.

4. When using a cable tensiometer to check cable tension, what practices help ensure an accurate reading?

5. During an annual inspection on a reciprocating engine you found a loose stud on the accessory drive section. You will remove the old stud and install an oversize stud. What kind of tap will you use to cut new threads in the new blind hole?

6. When drilling through aluminum sheets, what must you do to prevent elongating or oversizing the hole?

7. You are replacing a floor beam in a Boeing 757 aircraft. The Boeing Structural Repair Manual requires Hi-Lok fasteners with a 0.001" interference fit. How would you drill the holes?

8. Identify the major difference in the torqueing procedure when using a torque multiplier.

9. You are working inside a fuel tank on a Douglas DC-9 aircraft. You must drill out several fasteners to repair a fuel leak. However, the hangar is packed full, your DC-9 is parked far out on the ramp and you do not have enough air hoses to reach the aircraft. Another mechanic tells you to use a compressed nitrogen bottle to run your drill. What do you do?

10. Describe the difference between an inside micrometer and a telescoping gauge.

11. You are going to cut an aluminum flange with a hacksaw. Discuss the type of blade you would select and the proper use of the tool.

12. You are going to make a landing gear fairing for a light aircraft out of aluminum sheet, using sandbags and a hammer. What type of hammer should you select?

Chapter 4:
Tools and Techniques

ANALYSIS
QUESTIONS

name:

date:

Chapter 4:
Tools and Techniques

ANALYSIS QUESTIONS

name:

date:

13. You are removing the seat assemblies from a Boeing 727. In service, seat tracks become filled with food debris, candy, spilled beverages, and other material, which sometimes makes it difficult to get the seat assemblies out of the track. What type of hammer would you use to persuade the seats to move without harming their finish?

14. Name some of the measuring tools you would use to measure critical dimensions on a reciprocating engine piston and a cylinder assembly.

15. During an annual inspection on a reciprocating engine-powered light aircraft, you discover play in the carburetor's throttle shaft. The play is likely due to wear on the throttle shaft itself or on the throttle shaft bushings, which are pressed into the carburetor body. What measuring instruments would you use to determine which part(s) to replace?

16. In Question 15, suppose you found that the throttle shaft bushings were worn and needed replacement. You replaced the old bushings with new ones. What additional step would you perform to make sure that the throttle shaft does not leak when the carburetor is returned to service?

17. A recent OSHA study conducted in Austin, Texas over a seven year period provides a partial list of grinding wheel accidents. The report lists numerous lacerations, facial disfigurements, a number of finger amputations, and four fatalities. Discuss some precautions you will observe when working with or around grinding wheels.

18. When finding the thickness of a piece of sheet metal, why would you use a sheet metal/wire gauge instead of a caliper?

19. You want to determine the inside diameter of an aluminum duct. Discuss several different ways of doing this with different measuring tools, and identify the method (tool) that will give the most precise results.

20. After fabricating a replacement floor panel from honeycomb sheet, you apply an epoxy filler compound to the edge to seal the panel from moisture. What kind of file would you use to quickly remove excess compound from the edge and leave a smooth finish?

21. You are removing a section of sheet metal aircraft skin for a repair, and have drilled off the rivet heads. What tools would you use to remove the shanks?

22. You are overhauling a float carburetor, and the overhaul manual tells you to set the float level to 3/16 inch below the top edge mating surface. You could use a dial caliper, a six inch ruler, or a depth micrometer to set the float. Which should you use?

23. You are going to torque the six nuts that retain a hydraulic pump to an engine accessory drive. The required torque is 95 inch-pounds, and the torque wrench you checked out of the tool room has a range of 20 to 100 inch pounds. Can you use this wrench?

1. The most significant items in an airplane's construction are _____ .

2. Aircraft hardware is usually identified by its _____ or _____ .

3. The prefix MS identifies hardware that conforms to written _____ .

4. Letters following the head-shaped code on a rivet identify the _____ from which the rivet was made.

5. Rivets made of _____ alloy are used only for riveting nonstructural parts.

6. The _____ rivet is the most widely used rivet, especially in repair work.

7. The rivet in Question 6 is identified by a _____ head marking.

8. The 2017-T4 rivet has a _____ head marking.

9. A head marking of a _____ is on the 2024-T4 rivet.

10. Because of corrosion-resistant qualities, _____ rivets are used for joining magnesium alloy structures.

11. The self-plugging rivet includes the _____ and _____ in the rivet head.

12. Hi-shear rivets are used only in _____ .

13. Hi-shear rivets are never used where the _____ is less than the _____ .

14. _____ are used in structural applications because their shear and tensile strengths equal or exceed AN requirements.

15. A high strength blind structural fastener used when access to one side of the work is impossible is a _____ .

16. The threaded end of the pin of the _____ is recessed with a hexagon socket to allow installation from one side.

17. _____ fasteners are used to secure panels that require frequent removal.

18. The main difference between the two Dzus fasteners is a _____ , which is only used on the heavy-duty fasteners.

Chapter 5:
Hardware and Materials

FILL IN THE BLANK QUESTIONS

name:

date:

Chapter 5:
Hardware and
Materials

FILL IN THE BLANK
QUESTIONS

name:

date:

19. When assembling couplings or flanges that have been removed for maintenance, any seals and gaskets in the assembly should be _____ .

20. Whenever lines, components, or ducting are disconnected or removed, you should install suitable _____ , _____ or _____ on the openings.

21. A hose installed between two duct sections should have a gap between the duct ends of no less than _____ of an inch and no more than _____ of an inch.

22. The clamp on the connection in Question 21 should be _____ of an inch from the end of the connector and misalignment should not exceed _____ of an inch.

23. _____ are commonly used to secure hoses in ducting systems.

24. A flat-head pin should be secured with a _____ .

25. A snap ring is tempered to have a _____ action.

26. A _____ stud may be substituted for undersize or oversize studs.

27. _____ thread inserts are primarily designed to be used in materials that are not suitable for threading because of their softness.

28. A _____ is always designed to be turned by its head.

29. A _____ is generally tightened by turning the nut.

30. A right-hand thread on either a bolt or a screw advances into engagement when turned _____ .

31. A left-hand thread is indicated by the letters _____ following the class of thread.

32. The three principal parts of a bolt are the _____ , _____ , and _____ .

33. The diameter of the bolt is the thickness of its _____ .

34. The diameter is usually expressed as a whole number if the bolt is less than _____ of an inch thick.

35. The width and the thickness of the a bolt's _____ are also to be considered when choosing a bolt replacement.

36. A _____ has a round head and is used for shear applications.

37. The internal-wrenching bolt has a recessed _____ head and is tightened with a/an _____ wrench.

38. Bolt threads are either _____ or _____ and are not interchangeable.

39. When used in the part numbers for general-purpose AN bolts, clevis bolts and eyebolts, the letter "C" in the bolt material position means the bolt is made of _____ .

40. To signify that a bolt is not drilled for cotter pin safetying, the last character in its AN number is _____ .

41. Aircraft nuts all fall into two general groups: _____ and _____ .

42. A _____ is a nut that you can tighten with your fingers.

43. _____ nuts are used for blind mounting in inaccessible locations and for easier maintenance.

44. _____ screws can be used only in comparatively soft metals and materials.

45. The type of washer used where perfect alignment with the surface is required at all times is a _____ .

46. To make minor adjustments in cable length or to adjust cable tension, _____ are fitted in the cable assembly.

47. _____ are installed in cable assemblies for the purpose of making major adjustments in cable length and to compensate for cable stretch.

48. _____ protect cables from rubbing against nearby metal parts.

49. Quick-disconnect couplings are held together by a _____ .

50. Series 145 and 155 quick-disconnect couplings are properly tightened when there is a _____ minimum gap between the spring plate and the inside lip of the spring retainer fingers.

Chapter 5: *Hardware and Materials*

FILL IN THE BLANK QUESTIONS

name:

date:

Chapter 5:
Hardware and Materials

FILL IN THE BLANK
QUESTIONS

name:

date:

51. Newer compounds for hydraulic O-rings that improve low-temperature performance without sacrificing high-temperature performance have been developed with _____ .

52. The O-rings in Question 51 have an operating temperature range from _____ .

53. In hydraulic systems of _____ p.s.i. pressure or less, AN6227B, AN6230B, and MS28775 packings are used.

54. Normally, O-rings designated as MS28778 should be used only in connections with _____ .

55. O-rings found with _____ should not be used and should be removed from stock.

56. The _____ on the O-ring envelope indicates when the O-ring was manufactured.

57. Proper _____ are essential to protect O-rings from deformation, deterioration and contamination.

58. The _____ on hydraulic seals should not be removed until they are ready for installation.

59. After removal of all O-rings and before installing new ones, it is mandatory to _____ .

60. When O-ring installation requires inserting through sharp threaded areas, use protective measures such as _____ .

61. Two types of backup rings used to support O-rings in aircraft are _____ and _____ .

62. Once removed from its package, a new O-ring should first be _____ .

63. If possible, backup rings should be inserted _____ .

64. _____ are used to clean and lubricate the exposed portion of piston shafts.

65. Two types of protective metal closures approved for sealing hydraulic systems are _____ and _____ conforming to military specifications.

66. In all cases where there is a choice between internal or external installation of blank-off plates, use the _____ type of closure.

67. Electrical fittings or other non-fluid openings where contamination is not considered a problem may be sealed with _____ closures.

68. The process of connecting all the metal parts of an aircraft to complete an electrical circuit is called _____ .

69. Regardless of shape or material, all cotter pins are used for _____ .

70. The two approved methods of safetying turnbuckles are the _____ method and the preferred _____ .

Chapter 5:
Hardware and
Materials

FILL IN THE BLANK QUESTIONS

name:

date:

Chapter 5:
Hardware and Materials

**FILL IN THE BLANK
QUESTIONS**

name:

date:

1. Which of the following is **NOT** a production standard for aircraft materials and hardware?
   a. AN
   b. MS
   c. SAN
   d. SAE

2. Solid rivets are classified by:
   a. Size
   b. Material from which they are manufactured
   c. Head shape
   d. All of the above

3. Which number in the rivet identification code signifies the shank diameter?
   a. The first number after the specification code
   b. The first number after the alloy code
   c. The last number in the code
   d. It is the same number as the head shape

4. Which number in the rivet identification code signifies the rivet length?
   a. The first number after the specification code
   b. The first number after the alloy code
   c. The last number in the code
   d. It is the same number as the head shape

5. Which of the following rivet types may be substituted for 2017-T4 and 2024-T4 for repair work by using the next larger diameter?
   a. 1100-F
   b. 5056-H32
   c. 5056-H14
   d. 2117-T4

6. Which of these rivets must be driven within 20 minutes of heat treating or refrigerated at or below 32 degrees F?
   a. 2017-T4
   b. 2117-T4
   c. 2024-T4
   d. Both A and C

7. Where are blind rivets usually used?
   a. Places accessible from only one side
   b. To secure nonstructural parts to the airframe
   c. Where is space is too restricted to properly use a bucking bar
   d. All of the above

8. The shank diameter of a hi-shear rivet is measured in:
   a. Thirty-seconds of an inch
   b. Eighths of an inch
   c. Sixteenths of an inch
   d. Sixty-fourths of an inch

9. The grip length of a hi-shear rivet is measured in:
   a. Thirty-seconds of an inch
   b. Eighths of an inch
   c. Sixteenths of an inch
   d. Sixty-fourths of an inch

10. In sealed flotation or pressurized compartments, which type of rivet must be used?
    a. Closed-end rivnut
    b. Open-end rivnut
    c. Hi-shear rivet
    d. 1100-F rivet

Chapter 5:
Hardware and Materials

MULTIPLE CHOICE
QUESTIONS

name:

date:

Chapter 5:

Hardware and Materials

MULTIPLE CHOICE QUESTIONS

name:

date:

11. Which of the following is used in joints that carry shear loads and where the absence of clearance is essential?
    a. Flat-head pin
    b. Taper pin
    c. Safety pin
    d. Snap ring

12. In case of cotter pin failure the flat-head pin is normally installed with the head:
    a. Down
    b. Sideways
    c. Up
    d. It does not matter which way the head is because it is flat

13. Which of the following type of stud has a different thread on each end of the stud?
    a. Coarse thread
    b. Fine thread
    c. Stepped
    d. Snap thread

14. If the end of the threaded fastener is pointed, it is most likely a:
    a. Bolt
    b. Screw
    c. Stud
    d. None of the above

15. Correct length selection of a bolt is where the bolt extends through the nut at least:
    a. Three full threads
    b. Two full threads
    c. To the bottom of the grip
    d. None of the above

16. Grip length of the bolt should be approximately:
    a. The same as the thickness of the material to be fastened
    b. Longer than the thickness of the material to be fastened to allow for the nut
    c. Grip length does not matter, thread length does
    d. The same length as the threads

17. Which of these bolts must be installed with a special driver adapter?
    a. Hi-torque bolt
    b. Eye Bolt
    c. Clevis Bolt
    d. Close Tolerance Bolt

18. The material nuts are made of must be determined by:
    a. The number on the nut
    b. The number on the corresponding bolt
    c. The luster of the metal
    d. The size and shape of the nut

19. Which of these nuts is designed to be secured with cotter pins or safety wire?
    a. Castle nuts
    b. Self-locking nuts
    c. Barrel nuts
    d. None of the above

20. Which of these nuts is generally used where high tensile strength is required and space is limited?
    a. Plain hex nuts
    b. Channel nuts
    c. Internal-wrenching nuts
    d. Castle nuts

21. Which of the following nuts withstands temperature extremes and exposure to lubricants and weather?
    a. Klincher locknuts
    b. Sheet spring nuts
    c. Point-wrenching nuts
    d. Wing nuts

22. Which type of screw should never be used to replace standard screws, nuts or rivets in the original structure?
    a. Fillister-head
    b. Self-tapping
    c. Round-head
    d. Socket-head

23. Which of these screws is used in assembling highly stressed aircraft components?
    a. Truss-head
    b. Self-tapping
    c. Round-head
    d. Flush-head

24. Which of these cable characteristics is most common in aircraft cables?
    a. Right regular lay
    b. Left regular lay
    c. Left lang lay
    d. Right lang lay

25. Which type of cable guide is used for small openings in unpressurized compartments?
    a. Grommet
    b. Fairlead
    c. Pressure seal
    d. None of the above

26. Which of these allows the cable to move with a minimum of friction and wear?
    a. Fairlead
    b. Grommet
    c. Connector link
    d. Pulley

27. All quick disconnect couplings for aircraft hydraulics should be installed:
    a. With a wrench
    b. By hand
    c. In accordance with instructions in the manual
    d. With a full turn of the union nut

28. The series 3200 quick-disconnect coupling connection can be inspected by:
    a. Turning the union nut by hand in a clockwise direction
    b. Turning the union nut by hand in a counterclockwise direction
    c. Inspecting the locking female hex on the on the bulkhead coupling half
    d. None of the above

29. Tools used to remove O-rings and backup rings can be:
    a. Sharp
    b. Pointed
    c. Greased
    d. Made from plastic

30. Teflon backup rings:
    a. Are color coded.
    b. Deteriorate with age.
    c. Are unaffected by system fluid or vapor.
    d. Do not tolerate high temperatures.

Chapter 5:
Hardware and Materials

MULTIPLE CHOICE QUESTIONS

name:

date:

Chapter 5:
Hardware and Materials

31. To expand the ring diameter and reduce the possibility of damage when a Teflon spiral ring is installed in internal grooves, you should:
    a. Rotate the component in a counterclockwise direction
    b. Rotate the component in a clockwise direction
    c. Take care not to rotate the component at all
    d. Overlap the ring ends

32. To contract the ring diameter and reduce the possibility of damage when a Teflon spiral ring is installed in external grooves, you should:
    a. Rotate the component in a counterclockwise direction
    b. Rotate the component in a clockwise direction
    c. Take care not to rotate the component at all
    d. Overlap the ring ends

33. Which of the following is **NOT** considered a cable in aircraft electrical installations?
    a. Two or more insulated conductors in the same jacket
    b. A stranded conductor covered with insulating material
    c. An insulated conductor covered with a metallic braided shield
    d. A single insulated conductor with a metallic braided outer conductor

34. Most aircraft wire strands are held together with:
    a. Connectors
    b. Receptacle assembly
    c. Terminal lugs
    d. Twisted pairs

35. Static dischargers are used on aircraft to:
    a. Allow the satisfactory operation of onboard navigation systems
    b. Reduce the likelihood of the aircraft being struck by lightning
    c. Increase the potential static buildup on the aircraft
    d. Provide a low-resistance return path for single-wire electrical systems

36. Which of these is **NOT** secured by cotter pins?
    a. Bolts
    b. Terminal lugs
    c. Nuts
    d. All are secured by cotter pins

37. Which type of cotter pin can be used where nonmagnetic material is required?
    a. Stainless steel
    b. Low-carbon steel
    c. Plastic
    d. Iron

38. All nuts must be safetied except which type?
    a. Self-locking
    b. Plate nuts
    c. Castle nuts
    d. Pine nuts

39. There is no loop around the nut in safetying which type of nut?
    a. Castellated
    b. Shear
    c. Channel
    d. Plate

40. What type of safety wire is used for valves, levers or switches used for emergency operation of aircraft equipment?
    a. Annealed corrosion-resistant wire
    b. Insulated stainless steel wire
    c. Annealed copper wire
    d. Annealed aluminum wire

1. You are installing a landing gear door on a light aircraft using bolts, nuts and washers. The nuts must be safetied, but have poor access when they are installed. What kind of nut should you use in a situation like this? (Temperature is not a factor.)

2. What piece of hardware is preferred for carrying shear loads at joints with little or no clearance (play)?

3. What type of blind fastener would you consider to attach a sheetmetal skin to a stringer where interior access is poor?

4. What type of blind fastener would you consider to secure thick load-bearing structural members such as floor beams and stringers?

5. While blind rivets are acceptable for structural repairs and are easy to install, they are very expensive and should be used only when access to one side of the job is limited or impossible. What rivet would you select for an aluminum alloy repair to an aircraft skin? Assume you are away from the shop and heat-treating the rivets is not possible.

6. What type of rivet would you use for routine repairs to non-structural trim items in an aircraft galley structure?

7. What devices help control and dissipate electrical charges that build up in aircraft structures? What would you look for when inspecting them?

8. When replacing seals in a landing gear strut, what precautions would you take to ensure the strut does not leak when it is returned to service?

9. What would you look for when inspecting o-rings before you install them?

10. Describe how you would safety a turnbuckle.

11. What is different about the method you would use to safety a castle nut?

12. When is it acceptable to use an o-ring or backup ring that you found stored in an opened package?

13. What would you look for when inspecting a turnbuckle installation on a cable?

Chapter 5:
Hardware and Materials

ANALYSIS
QUESTIONS

name:

date:

Chapter 5:
Hardware and Materials

ANALYSIS
QUESTIONS

name:

date:

14. You are completing a coffee maker installation in an aircraft galley. You are going to bolt the coffee maker base to the galley cabinet structure, and want to make sure the grip length of the MS bolts you use is correct. How could you do this?

15. Describe how the process for installing 2117-T4 rivets differs from that of 2024-T4 rivets.

16. What limitations must you consider when considering the use of Hi-shear pin rivets?

17. A light aircraft engine cowl is secured to the airframe with screws. The aircraft owner wants this changed. What are your options? Assume that the question of major alteration is not an issue here.

18. While performing a 100 hour inspection on a reciprocating engine, you discover a spark plug hole has stripped threads. What can you do without replacing the cylinder head?

19. You find an aileron hinge bolt worn and want to replace it. You find a bolt in free stock that matches the old part's size and finish, but lacks identification marks on its head. Can you use it?

20. An aircraft battery is retained in the airframe by two hold-down clamps that are tightened by wing nuts, which are safety wired. You have lost one of the wing nuts. Can you substitute self-locking nuts in place of the wing nuts?

Chapter 6:
Fluid Lines and Fittings

FILL IN THE BLANK
QUESTIONS

name:

date:

1. Aircraft tubing has a _____ degree flare.

2. Tubing assemblies are used to transport _____ or _____ between various components of the aircraft system.

3. Outside diameter sizes of tubing are in _____ of an inch.

4. _____ tubing is used in high-pressure (3000 p.s.i.+) hydraulic systems.

5. When fabricating tube assemblies, always refer to the manufacturer's specifications for both _____ and _____ .

6. The objective in tube bending is to obtain a smooth bend without _____ the tube.

7. Due to varying elasticities of tubing, it may be necessary to bend the tube past the required bend to allow for _____ .

8. Before bending aluminum alloy tubing, pack it _____.

9. The flared end of a tube should be no larger than the _____ being used.

10. In preparing a flareless fitting, _____ is necessary to form the seal between the sleeve and the tube without damaging the _____ .

11. As a rule, beading machines are limited to use with tubing over _____ in diameter unless special rollers are supplied.

12. It is suggested that oxygen tubing be proof pressure tested using _____ and inspected for leaks by _____ .

13. Interior surfaces of airspeed indicator tubing, oxygen, or other plumbing lines should not be _____ .

14. Titanium or stainless steel tubing needs primer or paint in areas of _____ .

15. Any tube that carries physically dangerous material will be marked with tape displaying the letters _____ .

16. To aid in the rapid identification of the various tubing systems and operating pressures, each fluid line in the aircraft is identified by _____ .

17. Identification tape codes are applied in accordance with _____ and _____ , established to standardize fluid line identification throughout the industry.

Chapter 6:
Fluid Lines and Fittings

FILL IN THE BLANK QUESTIONS

name:

date:

18. When storing fabricated tubing and tube assemblies, do not use pressure-sensitive tape as a substitute for _____ .

19. Replace any aluminum, aluminum alloy, or steel tubing carrying pressures greater than _____ p.s.i. and with nicks or scratches greater than _____ percent of wall thickness.

20. Any dent that has a depth less than 20 percent of the tube diameter is acceptable unless the dent is on _____ .

21. When installing flareless tube assemblies, do not use pliers to tighten _____ .

22. In Question 21, a _____ wrench or _____ wrench should be used when tightening connections.

23. All hydraulic tubing adjacent to rigid structures should be supported by _____ .

24. Temporary tube repairs are made with splice sections fabricated with _____ or _____ .

25. _____ hose is compatible with phosphate ester hydraulic fluid.

26. In fabricating a hose assembly, the use of a special hand tool called a _____ will reduce the possibility of damaging the hose during installation of the nipple.

27. The FAA requires protective _____ installed over hose assemblies in areas where temperatures exceed the capabilities of the hose material.

28. When testing a hose assembly with an air or gas medium, test the assembly _____ so that trapped air can escape.

29. Hose assemblies with a _____ do not require the test described in Question 28.

30. All flexible hose manufactured in the shop must be _____ or _____ pressure tested prior to being installed in the aircraft.

31. In hose or hose assembly installations, proper _____ and _____ is mandatory.

32. A _____ hose or hose assembly must be replaced, while a _____ hose or hose assembly may be relieved by loosening clamps and swivel nuts and straightening by hand.

33. Do not attempt to straighten a _____ hose or hose assembly.

34. Do not use clamps with _____ cushioning unnecessarily as this type of cushioning material deteriorates rapidly when exposed to air.

35. If fluid used as a lubricant for fitting installation is not specified in the maintenance manual, use only the _____ .

36. A hose bent to a smaller radius than specified could become _____ .

37. Install hose or hose assemblies with a slight bow or slack to compensate for _____ .

38. When possible, install hose or hose assemblies so that _____ are visible.

39. A _____ refers only to the viability of the hose or hose assembly while in storage.

40. _____ means that as long as the hose or hose assembly can pass inspection it is airworthy.

41. _____ or _____ rubber hose and hose assemblies do not have shelf life limitations.

Chapter 6:
Fluid Lines and Fittings

FILL IN THE BLANK QUESTIONS

name:

date:

Chapter 6:
Fluid Lines and Fittings

FILL IN THE BLANK
QUESTIONS

name:

date:

1. Wall thickness of tubing is specified in:
   a. Tenths of an inch
   b. Hundredths of an inch
   c. Thousandths of an inch
   d. Inches

2. A number 10 tubing is has which outside diameter?
   a. 5/8 of an inch
   b. 3/4 of an inch
   c. 1/10 of an inch
   d. 1/2 of an inch

3. Which type of tubing is used for general purpose lines?
   a. Aluminum alloy
   b. Corrosion-resistant steel
   c. Titanium alloy
   d. Plastic

4. Which type of tube fitting is no longer used?
   a. MS
   b. AC
   c. AN
   d. CRES

5. Which of these tube fitting materials is color-coded blue?
   a. Titanium
   b. Carbon steel
   c. Aluminum alloy
   d. Corrosion-resistant steel

6. If a standard tube cutter is not available to cut tubing, use a:
   a. Fine-tooth hacksaw
   b. Diagonal cutting pliers
   c. Sharp scissors
   d. Utility knife

7. After tube deburring, the chamfer on the tube inside diameter (ID) should not exceed:
   a. One wall thickness of tubing
   b. One-half wall thickness of tubing
   c. One-quarter wall thickness of tubing
   d. Deburring will not affect the chamfer

8. Which of these on tubing can spread and split the tube when it is flared?
   a. Draw marks
   b. Square cuts
   c. Sand
   d. None of the above

9. Aluminum alloy tubing used in low-pressure oxygen systems is normally:
   a. Single-flared
   b. Double-flared
   c. Flareless
   d. Unflared

10. Corrosion-resistant steel tubing used in brake systems is normally:
    a. Tenths of an inch single-flared
    b. Double-flared
    c. Flareless
    d. Unflared

Chapter 6:

Fluid Lines and Fittings

MULTIPLE CHOICE QUESTIONS

name:

date:

Chapter 6:
Fluid Lines and Fittings

MULTIPLE CHOICE
QUESTIONS

name:

date:

11. As a guide, the pressure test for fabricated hose assemblies is at least how many times the system pressure?
    a. 1.5
    b. 2
    c. 4
    d. 1.25

12. Identification tags are applied to all lines less than 4 inches in diameter except:
    a. Cold lines
    b. Hot lines
    c. Lines in engine compartments
    d. All of the above

13. Instead of tags for identification, lines in oily environments are:
    a. Coated with clear varnish
    b. Etched
    c. Painted
    d. Stenciled

14. Which of these is **NOT** indicated by identification tape codes on a fluid line?
    a. Contents
    b. Pressure in the line
    c. Temperature
    d. Direction of flow

15. Which of these requires protection of the entire assembly when storing, in addition to protective closures at end fittings?
    a. Aluminum alloy flared tube assembly
    b. Oxygen tube assembly
    c. Steel flared tube assembly
    d. Hydraulic pressure line

16. If a steel flared tube assembly leaks, how much can it be tightened beyond the noted torque?
    a. One-sixteenth turn
    b. One-eighth turn
    c. One-half turn
    d. One complete turn only

17. Fittings that are damaged should be:
    a. Filed
    b. Cleaned
    c. Replaced
    d. Repaired in accordance with manufacturer's standards

18. An advantage of Teflon hose over synthetic rubber hose is:
    a. Its long life
    b. It normally comes in low-pressure types
    c. It is compatible with PTFE
    d. It is marked with the military specification number

19. Which material for flared hose fittings is color-coded black?
    a. Steel
    b. Aluminum
    c. Aluminum alloy
    d. Titanium alloy

20. When failures occur in hose assemblies equipped with reusable style and fittings, the fabrication of the replacement unit is the responsibility of:
    a. The manufacturer
    b. The Aviation Maintenance Technician
    c. The owner of the aircraft
    d. No one, as the unit is replaced with a new one

21. The first step in fabricating a hose assembly is:
    a. Determining the necessary hose length
    b. Determining the correct material to use
    c. Creating the identification tag
    d. Installing the nipple and nut assembly

22. A salvage hose of unknown age with a firesleeve may be contaminated with:
    a. Jet fuel
    b. Asbestos
    c. Hydraulic fuel
    d. Fiberglass

23. Preformed hose assemblies save:
    a. Time
    b. Money
    c. Reusable fittings
    d. Space

24. Unless specifically approved by the airframe manufacturer, using commercial soaps to clean fabricated hoses or hose assemblies could result in:
    a. Voiding the warranty
    b. Ineffective cleaning of the unit
    c. Damage to the hose material
    d. Corrosion

25. Before removing any hose or hose assembly:
    a. Determine the correct replacement hose or hose assembly
    b. Perform contamination control procedures
    c. Remove all supporting clamps
    d. Disconnect the assembly by using two open-ended wrenches

26. Protect preformed hose and hose assemblies from distortion with/by:
    a. Your hands
    b. Duct tape
    c. Tightening the clamps
    d. A restrainer

27. Minimum bend radii for hoses are contained in:
    a. The hose installation instructions
    b. The IPC
    c. FAA Advisory Circular 43.13-1B
    d. The hose manufacturer's information

28. Which of these will specify an acceptable number of broken wires on the hose braid?
    a. FAA Advisory Circular 43.13-1B
    b. The hose manufacturer's information
    c. The IPC
    d. The hose installation instructions

Chapter 6:
Fluid Lines and Fittings

MULTIPLE CHOICE QUESTIONS

name:

date:

Chapter 6:

Fluid Lines and Fittings

MULTIPLE CHOICE
QUESTIONS

name:

date:

29. A brownish coloration penetrating the outer braid of a hose with a carbon steel wire braid may indicate:
    a. It is really aluminum not carbon steel
    b. The hose is kinked
    c. Corrosion
    d. Fungus

30. Cushion-type clamps should be used on hoses to prevent:
    a. Chafing
    b. Flexing
    c. Twisting
    d. Warping

31. When connecting a hose or hose assembly to an engine or an engine-mounted accessory, how much slack should be between the last point of support and the engine or accessory attachment?
    a. 1 ½ inches
    b. 1 inch
    c. 1 ¾ inches
    d. There should be no slack

32. Operational life of hoses and hose assemblies is determined by:
    a. The hose manufacturer
    b. The aviation maintenance technician
    c. The aircraft manufacturer
    d. Passing an inspection

33. Hoses and hose assemblies should **NOT** be stored:
    a. Together
    b. In piles
    c. In a dark place
    d. In a cool place

34. Store hoses or hose assemblies so that:
    a. The largest are used first
    b. The smallest are easiest to get to
    c. The oldest are used first
    d. Air can circulate through the area

35. Which of these is **NOT** a test medium for proof pressure testing of hose assemblies?
    a. Water
    b. Oil
    c. Nitrogen
    d. Air

1. You need to cut a piece of aluminum tubing with a hacksaw. Describe the process.

2. What would you expect to have a shorter service life – a flex hose forward of an instrument panel, or a flex hose in an auxiliary power unit compartment? Why?

3. You are inspecting the nose landing gear hydraulic actuator mechanism on a light aircraft. What would you look for when inspecting the actuator's flexible hydraulic lines?

4. In question 3, assume you found a flex line worn beyond limits. You are going to fabricate a replacement hose in the shop. Describe how you would determine the length of the new hose, and what precaution you should observe when installing it.

5. You have fabricated a steel tubing assembly to be used in a pneumatic system. When pressure testing the assembly, you discover a leak at one of the tube nuts. What are some of the possible reasons for the leak?

6. You are given a piece of tubing for a low-pressure application and are told to fabricate a replacement. What additional information should you require?

7. What characteristics of beaded tubes most differentiate these tubes from flared-end tubes?

8. What determines if tube assemblies require paint or primer finishes?

9. What problems are caused by improper presetting of flareless fittings?

10. Most tube assembly leakage occurs at connectors. What other areas do you think should receive extra attention during an inspection to detect potential sources of leaks?

11. Describe three methods of repairing dents in tubing.

12. While preparing to reassemble a tube assembly in a hydraulic system you find an angle fitting with damaged threads. What repairs should you consider?

13. You must replace a piece of synthetic rubber hose. You find a piece in the stock room with only a partial part number, but the hose appears to be the correct material and diameter. Should you use it?

Chapter 6:

Fluid Lines and Fittings

ANALYSIS
QUESTIONS

name:

date:

Chapter 6:
Fluid Lines and Fittings

ANALYSIS
QUESTIONS

name:

date:

14. You fabricate a length of flex hose for a hydraulic system, but your shift ends before you clean and test it. Another technician on a different shift installs the hose and operates the hydraulic system. What should you do?

15. Inspecting a length of flex hose between two pieces of tubing, you notice deformation on the hose around one of the clamps (cold flow). Can you tighten the clamp to keep the joint from leaking?

1. Substances composed of only one type of atom are called _____.

2. Electron flow in a circuit is from _____ to _____.

3. A switch with two contactors (poles), each of which completes only one circuit is a

   _____ -pole _____ throw switch.

4. The electrolyte used in the Ni-Cad battery is a 30% solution (by weight) of

   _____ in distilled water.

5. The generator _____ rule can be used to determine the direction of the

   induced emf.

6. The two effects that occur in an AC circuit (current direction and magnitude constantly

   changing) that do not occur in a DC circuit are _____ reactance

   and _____ reactance.

7. _____ are light-activated variable resistors.

8. _____ is the process of changing AC to DC.

9. The ratio between true power and apparent power is expressed as the_____.

10. The factor that determines whether a transformer is a step-up or step-down type is the

    _____ .

11. An _____ is basically an amplifier circuit that has been modified

    slightly to allow it to generate an output waveform.

12. Aircraft electrical circuits require _____ type circuit breakers, which

    are designed to open regardless of the position of their operating control.

13. Wire diameters become _____ as the gauge numbers become

    _____ .

14. _____ and _____ are the two types of variable re-

    sistors that are constructed of a circular resistance material over which a sliding contact moves.

15. The first and the second color bands on a resistor are never _____

    or _____ in color.

16. If a resistor has no fourth color band, the tolerance is understood to be

    _____ percent.

17. _____ circuits are circuits in which two or more electrical resistances,

    or loads, are connected across the same voltage source.

Chapter 7:

Basic Electricity

FILL IN THE BLANK QUESTIONS

name:

date:

Chapter 7:
Basic Electricity

FILL IN THE BLANK
QUESTIONS

name:

date:

18. A battery cell is a device that converts _____ energy into _____ energy.

19. Lead-acid batteries have cells with positive plates of _____ and negative plates of _____ .

20. The state of charge of a lead-acid battery is indicated by the density of the electrolyte and is checked using a _____ .

21. The depth to which the hydrometer sinks into the electrolyte is determined by the electrolyte's density, or _____ .

22. A specific gravity reading between _____ indicates a high state of charge.

23. The electrolyte in Ni-Cad batteries is _____ to the sulphuric acid used in a lead-acid battery.

24. The three elements of a triode vacuum tube are the _____ , _____ , and _____ .

25. In a transistor circuit, the electrical potential applied from the battery to the electrodes of the transistor diodes is called _____ .

26. The _____ was originally developed to replace incandescent bulbs in indicator light circuits.

27. An _____ differs from a conventional diode in that it will not begin conduction until a certain minimum voltage is exceeded, or until a voltage is applied to the gate terminal.

28. The basic DC meter movement used in many types of electrical test equipment is known as the _____ .

29. In order to measure the voltage drop across a resistor, voltage-measuring instruments should be connected _____ (in parallel with) the resistor.

30. The ohmmeter is widely used to measure resistance and to check the _____ of electrical circuits and devices.

31. An _____ in a series circuit causes current flow to stop.

32. A _____ in a series circuit produces greater-than-normal current.

33. A shorted circuit may eventually produce an _____ by blowing (opening) the fuse, burning out a circuit component, or tripping the circuit breaker.

34. AC motors have a number of advantages over DC motors, the main ones being _____ , _____ , and _____ .

35. Induction motors have a rotor that is called the _____ .

36. The synchronous speed of an induction motor is the speed at which the magnetic field rotates and it depends upon the number of _____ for which the stator is wound and the _____ of the applied voltage.

Chapter 7:

Basic Electricity

FILL IN THE BLANK QUESTIONS

name:

date:

Chapter 7:

Basic Electricity

FILL IN THE BLANK QUESTIONS

name:

date:

1. Which Bell Lab scientist invented the transistor in 1948?
   a.   John Bardeen
   b.   Walter Brattain
   c.   William Shockley
   d.   All of the above

2. Electrical wiring may be made from many different types of metal. Of the four metals listed, the best conductor material is:
   a.   Copper.
   b.   Silver
   c.   Aluminum
   d.   Steel

3. If the cross-sectional area of a conductor is doubled, the resistance to current flow will be what amount of the original resistance?
   a.   Twice as much
   b.   Half as much
   c.   The same
   d.   78.6% of the original amount.

4. A lead-acid battery cell contains positive plates coated with:
   a.   Lead
   b.   Chromium
   c.   Zinc
   d.   Lead Peroxide

5. In theory, a 100-ampere battery will furnish:
   a.   100 amperes for one hour
   b.   50 amperes for two hours
   c.   20 amperes for five hours
   d.   All of the above

6. The most commonly used reversible type motor in aircraft is:
   a.   Reversible series
   b.   Reversible shunt
   c.   Reversible compound
   d.   Reversible torque

7. Field-effect transistors are also known as:
   a.   Petticoat junction transistors
   b.   Matching impedance transistors
   c.   Bipolar junction transistors
   d.   Threshold junction transistors

8. When using a megger, always observe the following safety precautions:
   a.   Use leather gloves
   b.   Use only for high-resistance measurements
   c.   Never use on an aircraft if conditions do not absolutely require it.
   d.   Answers B and C

9. The SCR (silicone-controlled rectifier) has what number of electrodes?
   a.   Four
   b.   Three
   c.   Five
   d.   One

10. SCR (silicone-controlled rectifier) electrodes are labeled:
    a.   Drain, Gate, Source
    b.   Anode, Cathode, Tetrode
    c.   Cathode, Gate, Anode
    d.   Emitter, Base, Collector

Chapter 7:

Basic Electricity

MULTIPLE CHOICE QUESTIONS

name:

date:

Chapter 7:

Basic Electricity

MULTIPLE CHOICE
QUESTIONS

name:

date:

11. The grid in a triode vacuum tube controls electron flow between the:
    a. Grid and anode
    b. Anode and the pentode
    c. Plate and the socket
    d. Cathode and the plate

12. The ratio between true power and apparent power is expressed as the power factor and may be found by dividing:
    a. Circuit resistance by current flow in amperes
    b. True voltage by current in the circuit
    c. Circuit resistance by impedance
    d. Average power by true power

13. The formula for finding impedance (total opposition to current flow in an AC circuit) can be found by using:
    a. The law of right triangles
    b. Pythagorean theorem
    c. Both A and B
    d. None of the above

14. In a solid state diode, current flow will increase if:
    a. Forward bias is decreased
    b. Forward bias is increased
    c. Thermal bias is reversed
    d. Bias becomes excessive

15. If an AC voltage is applied to the primary of an iron core transformer, the iron core will be magnetized and demagnetized at the same frequency as that of the:
    a. Applied Current
    b. Induced amplification
    c. Applied voltage
    d. None of the above

16. For all induction motors, the principle of operation is a:
    a. Rotating magnetic field
    b. Rotating polarity
    c. Rotating slip rings
    d. Rotating coils

17. The squirrel cage rotor in an induction motor has a speed of rotation determined by:
    a. Number of poles in the field winding
    b. Frequency of the applied voltage
    c. Both A and B
    d. None of the above

18. In a step-down transformer, the resistance of the secondary winding will be:
    a. More than that of the primary winding
    b. The same as that of the primary winding
    c. Less than that of the primary winding
    d. Twice as much as the primary winding

19. If a transformer winding is completely short-circuited, several things may occur if power is applied:
    a. The transformer overheats
    b. The voltage reading across the secondary is zero
    c. Strong burnt odor.
    d. All of the above

20. Microswitches are used primarily as:
    a. Light switches
    b. Radio switches
    c. Limit switches
    d. Momentary switches

21. A resistor having the value of 2700 ohms would be color coded this way:
    a. First band blue, second band brown, third band green
    b. First band red, second band violet, third band red
    c. First band yellow, second band violet, third band green
    d. First band red, second band violet, third band green

22. Circuits in which two or more loads are connected across the same voltage source are called:
    a. Series
    b. Control
    c. Parallel
    d. Complex

23. Which statement is **NOT** true when using the constant current method for recharging a battery?
    a. The current remains almost constant.
    b. This method requires a longer time to charge a battery fully.
    c. Toward the end of the process, care must be exercised to prevent the danger of overcharging.
    d. Constant-current chargers cannot be used to charge more than one battery at a time

24. When a storage battery is being charged, what two gases are generated?
    a. Oxygen and nitrogen
    b. Sulphur dioxide and oxygen
    c. Hydrogen and oxygen
    d. Carbon dioxide and oxygen

25. A battery's state of charge is indicated by:
    a. A hygrometer
    b. Density of the electrolyte
    c. A hydrometer
    d. Both B and C

26. To reverse the direction of rotation in a DC motor:
    a. Reverse the direction of current in the armature windings.
    b. Reverse the direction of current in the field windings.
    c. Reverse the direction of current in the armature windings and field windings.
    d. Reverse the direction of current in the armature windings or the field windings.

27. A cumulative compound motor has both a series field and a shunt field. The purpose of the shunt field is to:
    a. Regulate counter-electromotive force
    b. Maintain full rotor speed under high load conditions
    c. Prevent the motor from running away under a no-load condition
    d. Threshold junction transistors

28. Looking at Figure 7-19-19, which of the following statements is true?
    a. R3 becoming open-circuited would cause the fuse to blow.
    b. R2 becoming short-circuited would cause the fuse to blow.
    c. R1 becoming open-circuited and R3 becoming short-circuited would cause the fuse to blow.
    d. R1 becoming short-circuited and R3 becoming open-circuited would cause the fuse to blow.

Chapter 7:

Basic Electricity

MULTIPLE CHOICE QUESTIONS

name:

date:

Chapter 7:
Basic
Electricity

MULTIPLE CHOICE
QUESTIONS

name:

date:

29. Zener diodes are used primarily for:
    a. Voltage regulation
    b. Current regulation
    c. Rectification
    d. Positive bias

30. The emitter, base, and collector in a junction transistor correspond to which parts in a triode vacuum tube?
    a. Cathode, grill and plate
    b. Screen grid, heater and plate
    c. Cathode, grid, and plate
    d. Diode, plate, and heater

31. Photo diodes are light-activated variable:
    a. Transistors
    b. Resistors
    c. Switches
    d. Transformers

32. The electrodynamometer can be used to measure:
    a. AC voltage
    b. DC voltage
    c. Current
    d. All of the above

33. A bridge-type, full-wave rectifier has:
    a. Two diodes
    b. No diodes
    c. Four diodes
    d. Three diodes

34. Capacitors may also be known by this older, outdated term:
    a. DC blocker
    b. AC blocker
    c. Condenser
    d. Both A and C

35. The synchronous speed of an induction motor is found by:
    a. Multiplying the frequency by 60 and dividing the result by half the number of poles per phase
    b. Multiplying the frequency by 60 and dividing the result by the number of poles per phase
    c. Multiplying the voltage by 60 and dividing the result by half the number of poles per phase
    d. Multiplying the voltage by 60 and dividing the result by the number of poles per phase

36. Rheostats and potentiometers are examples of:
    a. Variable transistors
    b. Transformers
    c. Variable resistors
    d. Capacitors

Chapter 7:
Basic
Electricity

FILL IN THE BLANK
QUESTIONS

name:

date:

1. You are replacing a resistor that has become blackened from overheating in a circuit and you cannot determine its value from the obscured color bands. Checking the schematic, you see that a 3.9K ohm resistor with a five percent tolerance is required, so you select a resistor with an _____ first color band, a _____ second color band, a _____ third color band, and a _____ fourth color band.

2. Looking at figure 7-6-5 , compute the current and voltage drop across R1 and R2. The battery is 28 volts, R1 is 40 ohms and R2 is 100 ohms. When the switch is closed, _____ amps will flow in the circuit, R1 experiences an _____ volt drop and R2 experiences a _____ volt drop.

3. When the input voltage and turns ratio of a transformer is known, the transformer output voltage can be determined. If the input voltage is 120 volts, the primary has 100 turns and the secondary has 50 turns, you expect the output voltage to be _____ , making this transformer a step-_____ transformer.

4. The total resistance to current flow in AC (alternating current) circuits is called impedance, which is the combination of inductive reactance, capacitive reactance, and resistance. Using the formula for determining total resistance in a circuit with X_C of 5 ohms, X_L of 10 ohms, R of 100 ohms, you would expect total resistance to be approximately (rounded off to the nearest hundredth) _____ ohms.

5. If you are installing an aural warning device in the cockpit and the device manufacturer limits resistance of the wire run to one ohm, you determine from the American Wire Gauge Chart (Table 7-5-2) that you must use at least a _____ gauge wire or larger for a run of 90 feet.

6. You are using a hydrometer to check the specific gravity of a lead-acid battery and the reading indicated is 1.270. The electrolyte temperature is 101°F, so you expect the adjusted specific gravity reading to be _____ and the battery to be in a _____ state of charge.

Chapter 7:
Basic Electricity

**FILL IN THE BLANK
QUESTIONS**

name:

date:

1. While charging a nickel-cadmium battery at a constant 28.5 (± 0.1) volts, current does not drop below one amp after a 30-minute charge. Is there a problem and if so, what is the likely cause? Furthermore, what would you do to correct the condition?

2. Assume you are opening your own maintenance shop. Why should you separate the battery shop into two rooms, one for Ni-Cad battery maintenance, and one for Lead-Acid battery maintenance?

3. LED's (light-emitting diodes) may be a better choice for use as warning indicator lights in certain aircraft systems than incandescent bulbs. Name several reasons why:

4. What feature of a series motor makes it ideal for use as a starter and actuator?

5. What two ways may the speed of a shunt-wound motor be controlled?

6. How is the rotational speed of the squirrel-cage rotor controlled in an induction motor?

7. Why should you never use an ohmmeter to check continuity of a circuit that includes fire extinguisher bottle squibs (bottle firing devices)?

8. You are troubleshooting a circuit that requires the use of a voltmeter. Electrically speaking, how would you connect the voltmeter and why?

9. You are troubleshooting a warning light circuit that consists of an LED, normally triggered on by an SCR. The LED does not illuminate when conditions are present that should cause it to flash on. You have determined that the LED is good, the supply voltage is correct, and the SCR gate is receiving the correct signal voltage. What do you suspect may be the cause of the problem?

10. One type of full wave rectifier circuit consists of a center-tapped transformer, two diodes, and a load resistor. What purpose does the load resistor serve?

11. What is the apparent power in a reactive circuit carrying 5 amps at 28 volts?

12. What effect does inductive reactance and capacitive reactance have on current and voltage in an AC circuit?

Chapter 7:
Basic
Electricity

ANALYSIS
QUESTIONS

name:

date:

Chapter 7:
Basic Electricity

ANALYSIS
QUESTIONS

name:

date:

1. At any given time, a binary function can be in only _____ of _____ possible states.

2. A function is defined as _____ .

3. An input to a function is sufficient only if the input is within the _____ .

4. The output of a function is considered to be sufficient only if the output is within the _____ .

5. The truth table displays each possible combination of _____ to the function/system and the resultant _____ for that input.

6. The logical operator of a function is defined as the logical relationship between the _____ .

7. The truth table for the input/output relationships of a function with six inputs would contain entries for exactly _____ configurations of these inputs.

8. Identify each logical operator in the space beneath its symbol.

9. The following truth table represents a/an _____ logical operator.

A	B	OUTPUT
1	1	1
1	0	1
0	1	1
0	0	0

10. The following truth table represents a/an _____ logical operator.

A	B	OUTPUT
1	1	0
1	0	1
0	1	1
0	0	0

Chapter 8:
Binary Logic

FILL IN THE BLANK QUESTIONS

name:

date:

Chapter 8:
Binary Logic

FILL IN THE BLANK QUESTIONS

name:

date:

11. The following truth table represents a/an _____ logical operator.

A	B	OUTPUT
1	1	0
1	0	1
0	1	1
0	0	1

12. The following truth table represents a/an _____ logical operator.

A	B	OUTPUT
1	1	1
1	0	0
0	1	0
0	0	0

13. For a NAND logical operator, the output will be high if, and only if, _____ .

14. An electrical wire or a hydraulic line can be represented by the _____ logical operator symbol.

15. Consider a system in which hydraulic pressure is provided by two hydraulic pumps, either of which will provide sufficient pressure for the system. The logic of this function of the system can be described by a/an _____ logical operator.

16. Assume a function with the following specification:
    a. There are two inputs (A and B) and one output (C).
    b. If Input A is high and Input B is low, then the output is high.
    c. If Input A is high and Input B is high, then the output is low.
    d. If Input A is low and Input B is low, then the output is low.
    e. If Input A is low and Input B is high, then the output is high.

    This function has a/an _____ logical operator.

17. Assume a function with the following specification:
    a. There are two inputs (A and B) and one output (C).
    b. If Input A is high and Input B is low, then the output is low.
    c. If Input A is high and Input B is high, then the output is low.
    d. If Input A is low and Input B is low, then the output is high.
    e. If Input A is low and Input B is high, then the output is low.

    This function has a/an _____ logical operator.

18. Consider the binary number 11111111 that contains eight bits (one byte). The least significant bit is the bit located _____ .

19. In mathematics, the value of any positive number raised to the zero power (any positive number with 0 as its exponent) is _____ .

20. The number 10101 in the Base 2 binary system can be converted to _____ in the Base 10 decimal system.

Chapter 8:
Binary
Logic

FILL IN THE BLANK
QUESTIONS

name:

date:

21. The number 1101 in the Base 2 binary system can be converted to

_____ in the Base 10 decimal system or _____

in the Base 16 hexadecimal system.

22. Assume a system whose configuration is controlled by a six-bit binary digital device.
The maximum number of configurations that can be controlled by this device is

_____ .

23. Maintenance technicians often receive malfunction reports from the system operators. When
troubleshooting the system, the technician must confirm whether the reported malfunction is
valid (an actual fault) by _____ .

24. Consider a function with three inputs that has an AND logical operator. A test indicates that
the output is low (not sufficient). The technician can assume that the function has failed if,
and only if, _____ .

25. Consider a function with an XOR logical operator. Tests indicate that one input is high, the
other input is low and the output is low. With this information, what should the technician
conclude about the function? _____

26. Consider a function that has an XOR logical operator. Tests indicate that its output is low
(not sufficient) when both inputs are high (sufficient). Does this indicate that the function has
failed (yes/no)? _____

A	B	OUTPUT
1	1	0
1	0	0
0	1	0
0	0	1

27. You are asked to develop a truth table for a function that has eight inputs. How many
configurations of input and output must you include? _____

28. The following truth table represents a/an _____ logical operator.

29. Within a network of functions, the output of each function has an affect upon the behavior
of the next function downstream of it. In troubleshooting, these paths are called

_____ .

30. For the function F1 shown below, Input A = 28 volts, Input B = 28 volts, and Output C = 0.
From this information, can it be inferred that the function has failed?

A → [F1] → C
B →

Chapter 8:
Binary Logic

FILL IN THE BLANK QUESTIONS

name:

date:

NOTE: *In the analysis of all systems, assume single faults only. Also assume that functions always fail to the low output state.*

Chapter 8:
Binary
Logic

1. The highest value digit in the octal number system is:
   a. 2
   b. 4
   c. 7
   d. 8

2. The highest value digit in the hexadecimal number system is:
   a. 2
   b. 8
   c. E
   d. F

3. The value of x^0 (the number x raised to the zero power) is:
   a. 0
   b. 1 if the value of x is greater than 0
   c. 8 in the octal number system
   d. 2 in the binary number system

4. The value of the binary number 11100 converted to the decimal number system is:
   a. 11,100
   b. 111
   c. 28
   d. 56

5. The number 256 in the decimal system can be converted to the hexadecimal number:
   a. FF
   b. F
   c. 16
   d. 11111111

6. If a function has an AND logical operator, its output will be sufficient if, and only if:
   a. All inputs are sufficient
   b. All inputs are low
   c. At least one input is sufficient
   d. At least one input is not sufficient

7. The following symbol is for a function with:
   a. An AND logical operator
   b. A NOR logical operator
   c. A NAND logical operator
   d. An XOR logical operator

8. Which of the following symbols is correct for a NOR logical operator:

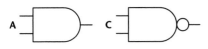

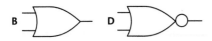

MULTIPLE CHOICE QUESTIONS

name:

date:

9. Two functions are combined to form a higher function as shown below. The logical operator of the combined function is a/an:
    a. AND
    b. NAND
    c. OR
    d. NOR

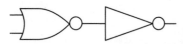

10. The following truth table is for a/an:
    a. OR logical operator
    b. NOR logical operator
    c. AND logical operator
    d. NAND logical operator

A	B	OUTPUT
1	1	1
1	0	1
0	1	1
0	0	0

11. The following truth table is for a/an:
    a. OR logical operator
    b. NOR logical operator
    c. AND logical operator
    d. NAND logical operator

A	B	OUTPUT
1	1	0
1	0	1
0	1	1
0	0	1

12. The following truth table is for a/an:
    a. OR logical operator
    b. NOR logical operator
    c. AND logical operator
    d. NAND logical operator

A	B	OUTPUT
1	1	1
1	0	0
0	1	0
0	0	0

13. For the system shown below, Output C should be:
    a. Low if Inputs A and B are both low
    b. Low if Inputs A and B are both high
    c. Low if Input A is low and Input B is high
    d. Low if Input A is high and Input B is low

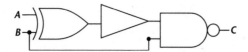

Chapter 8:

*Binary
Logic*

MULTIPLE CHOICE
QUESTIONS

name:

date:

14. For the system shown below, Output C should be
    a.   Low if Inputs A and B are both low
    b.   Low if Inputs A and B are both high
    c.   Low if Input A is low and Input B is high
    d.   Low if Input A is high and Input B is low

15. In this system, the output from F8 is low and the output from F9 also is low. Failure of what function(s) could cause this fault?
    a.   F7 only
    b.   F1, F2, F5, F6 or F7
    c.   F5 or F7
    d.   F5, F6 or F7

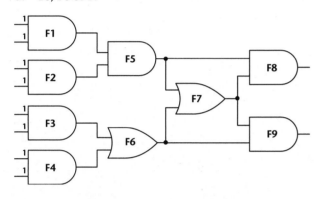

16. In the system shown in Question 15, the output from F8 is high and the output from F9 is low. Failure of what function(s) could cause this fault?
    a.   F6, F7 or F9
    b.   F6 or F9
    c.   F6 only
    d.   F9 only

17. In the system shown in Question 15, the output from F8 is low and the output from F9 is high. Failure of what function(s) could cause this fault?
    a.   F8 only
    b.   F5 or F8
    c.   F5, F7 or F8
    d.   F1, F2, F5, or F8

18. In this system, the output from F8 is low and the output from F9 also is low. Failure of what function(s) could cause this fault?
    a.   F7 only
    b.   F5 or F6
    c.   F6 only
    d.   F1, F2, F5, F6 or F7

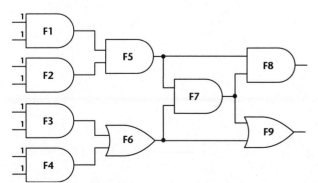

Chapter 8:
Binary
Logic

MULTIPLE CHOICE
QUESTIONS

name:

date:

19. In the system shown in Question 18, the output from F8 is high and the output from F9 is low. Failure of what function(s) could cause this fault?
    a. F9 only
    b. F7 or F9
    c. F6 only
    d. F6, F7 or F9

20. In the system shown in Question 18, the output from F8 is low and the output from F9 is high. Failure of what function(s) could cause this fault?
    a. F8 only
    b. F1, F2, F5, F8
    c. F1, F2, F6, F7, F8
    d. F1, F2, F5, F6, F7, F8

21. In the system shown for this Question, the output from F7 is high and the output from F8 is low regardless of switch position. Failure of what function(s) could cause this fault?
    a. F1, F2, F5 or Switch S1
    b. F1, F2, F5, Switch S1 or F8
    c. Switch S1 or F8
    d. F8 only

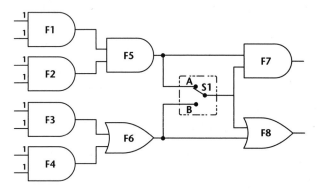

22. In the system shown for Question 21, when the switch is in position A, the outputs from both F7 and F8 are high. When the switch is in position B, the outputs from both F7 and F8 are low. Failure of what function(s) could cause this fault?
    a. F1, F2, F5, F6 or Switch S1
    b. F6 or the B position of Switch S1
    c. F6 only
    d. F6, B position of Switch S1, or F8

23. In the system shown for Question 21, when the switch is in position A, the output from F7 is low and the output from F8 is high. When the switch is in position B, the outputs from both F7 and F8 are high. Failure of what function(s) could cause this fault?
    a. F1, F2, F5, F7 or position A of Switch S1
    b. F1, F2, F5, or position A of Switch S1
    c. F1, F2 or F5
    d. F5 only

24. In the system shown for Question 21, the output from F7 is low and the output of F8 is high, regardless of switch position. Failure of what function(s) could cause this fault?
    a. F7 only
    b. Switch S1 only
    c. F7 or Switch S1
    d. Position A of Switch S1 only

Chapter 8:
Binary
Logic

MULTIPLE CHOICE
QUESTIONS

name:

date:

25. In this system, the output of F13 is low. The outputs of F14, F15 and F16 are high. Failure of what function(s) could cause this fault?
    a.   F2, F3, F4, F5, F7, F8, F9, F11 or F12
    b.   F7 or F14
    c.   F13 only
    d.   F1, F2, F3, F6, F7, F8, F10, F14

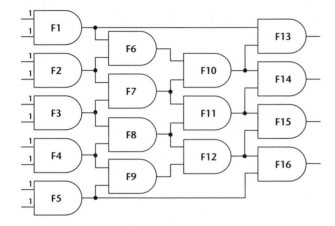

26. In the system shown in Question 25, the outputs from F13 and F14 are high. The outputs from F15 and F16 are low. Failure of what function(s) could cause this fault?
    a.   F2, F3, F4, F5, F7, F8, F9 or F12
    b.   F8, F9 or F12
    c.   F5 or F9
    d.   F5, F9 or F12

27. In the system shown in Question 25, the outputs from F13, F14 and F15 are high. The output from F16 is low. Failure of what function(s) could cause this fault?
    a. F16 only
    b. F5, F9 or F16
    c. F5, F9, F12, or F16
    d. F3, F4, F5, F8, F9, F12 or F16

28. In this system, the output from F15 is low. The outputs from F13, F14 and F16 are high. Failure of what function(s) could cause this fault?
    a.   F15 only
    b.   F8, F11 or F15
    c.   F4, F8, F11 or F15
    d.   F8, F11, F12 or F15

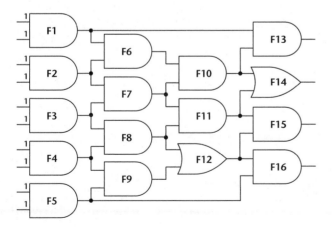

**MULTIPLE CHOICE
QUESTIONS**

name:

date:

29. In the system shown in Question 28, the output from F16 is low. The outputs from F13, F14 and F15 are high. Failure of what function(s) could cause this fault?
    a. F16 only
    b. F12 or F16
    c. F5 or F16
    d. F5, F9, F12 or F16

30. In the system shown in Question 28, the outputs from F15 and F16 are low. The outputs from F13 and F14 are high. Failure of what function(s) could cause this fault?
    a. F4, F5, F8, F9, F11 or F12
    b. F5 only
    c. F12 only
    d. F4 or F1

NOTE: *In the analysis of all systems, assume single faults only. Also assume that functions always fail to the low output state.*

1. The following combination of logical operators is equivalent to one

   _____ type logic gate.

    =

2. Construct a truth table for the following combination of logic gates.

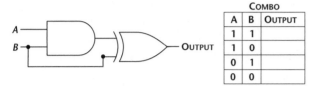

COMBO		
A	B	OUTPUT
1	1	
1	0	
0	1	
0	0	

3. For the system shown below, which function(s) can fail and the F7 output will still be high?

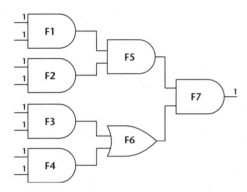

4. For the system shown below, tests indicate a low output from F5 and F7. Failure of what function(s) could be causing this situation?

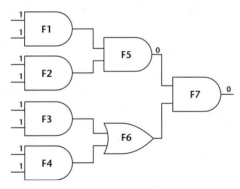

5. In the system shown below, failure of what function(s) could cause the failed output from F7?

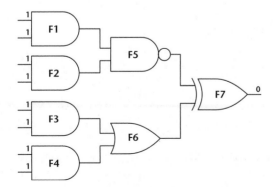

Chapter 8:
Binary Logic

ANALYSIS
QUESTIONS

name:

date:

6. In the system shown in Question 5, tests indicate a low output from F5 and a high output from F6. The output from F7 is low. Failure of what function(s) could cause the low output from F7?

7. In the system shown in Question 5, failure of what function(s) could cause a high output from F5?

8. In the system shown below, what should be the output from Function F7 if Function F6 failed to a low output?

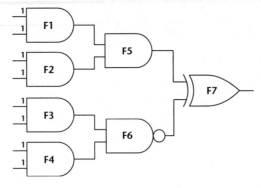

9. In the system shown in Question 8, failure of what function(s) could cause a low output from Function F7?

10. Again consider the system shown in Question 8: why would a failure of Function F6 not cause a low output from Function F7?

11. In the system shown in Question 8, tests indicate that the output from F5 is low and the output from F7 also is low. Failure of what function(s) could cause this situation?

12. Complete the truth table for the system shown below.

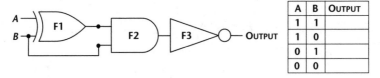

A	B	OUTPUT
1	1	
1	0	
0	1	
0	0	

13. Complete the truth table for the system shown below.

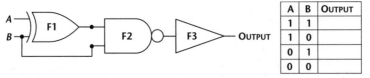

A	B	OUTPUT
1	1	
1	0	
0	1	
0	0	

14. In the system shown in Question 13, assume that Function F1 fails to the low output state. Complete the following truth table for that situation.

A	B	OUTPUT
1	1	
1	0	
0	1	
0	0	

15. Complete the truth table for the system shown below.

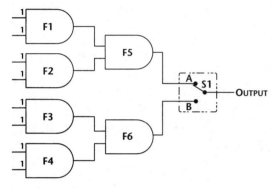

A	B	OUTPUT
1	1	
1	0	
0	1	
0	0	

ANALYSIS QUESTIONS

name:

16. The logical operator of the entire system shown in Question 15 is the same as the logical operator of a single _____ gate.

date:

17. In the system shown below, the output from Switch S1 is high when the switch is in Position A and low when the switch is in Position B. Failure of which function(s) could cause this situation?

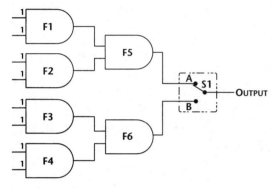

18. In the situation described in Question 17, a test indicates that the output of F6 is low. What new information is gained from this test?

19. In the system shown in Question 17, how will a low output from Function F2 affect the output from Switch S1?

20. In the system shown below, the output from Function F7 should be _____ when Switch S1 is in the A position and _____ when the switch is in the B position.

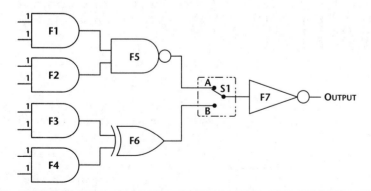

21. In the system shown in Question 20, the output from Function F7 is high when the Switch S1 is in the A position and low when the switch is in the B position. Failure of what function(s) could cause this fault?

Chapter 8:

Binary Logic

ANALYSIS
QUESTIONS

name:

date:

22. In the system shown in Question 20, the output from Function F7 is low when Switch S1 is in either position. Failure of what function(s) could cause this fault?

23. In normal operation of the system shown below with Switch S1 in the A position, Output #1 is _____ and Output #2 is _____ .

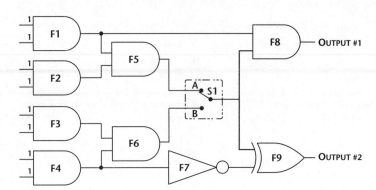

24. In normal operation of the system shown in Question 23 with Switch S1 in the B position, Output #1 is _____ and Output #2 is _____ .

25. In the system shown in Question 23, with the switch in the A position, Output #1 is low and Output #2 is low. Failure of what function(s) could cause this fault.

FILL IN THE BLANK QUESTIONS

name:

date:

1. The earliest form of language used to communicate information and ideas was _____ .

2. _____ is the drawing of an engineering picture of an object.

3. Never make a layout directly from a copy of the engineering drawing because copies can _____ .

4. A _____ drawing supplies complete information for the construction of a single part.

5. An electrical block diagram does not show _____ .

6. An understanding of _____ is necessary to interpret logic flow charts.

7. In orthographic projection drawings, there is/are _____ possible view/views of an object.

8. _____ drawings cannot be used to express complex parts.

9. Line intensities may vary somewhat on different drawings but there will always be a noticeable difference between a _____ and a _____ line.

10. Solid lines with one arrowhead indicate a part or portion to which a _____ , _____ , or other _____ applies.

11. _____ lines indicate the type of material from which the object is made.

12. _____ is the acceptable variation from the specific dimension given on a print or drawing.

13. In dimensioning distances between holes in an object, dimensions are usually given from _____ to _____ of the holes.

14. In limit dimensioning on a drawing, the _____ limit is place above the _____ limit.

15. The dimensions given for fits signify the amount of _____ allowed between moving parts.

16. A _____ allowance in Question 15 is given for a force or interference fit.

17. A _____ allowance in Question 15 is given for a part that is to revolve upon another part.

Chapter 9:
Blueprints and Drawings

FILL IN THE BLANK
QUESTIONS

name:

date:

18. _____ is the description for usage of various diagrams.

19. The universal numbering system provides a means of identifying standard drawing _____ .

20. Revisions to a drawing are necessitated by changes in _____ , _____ , or _____ .

21. Zone numbers on drawings are to help locate a _____ .

22. Buttock line stations are measured in inches from the _____ of the aircraft.

23. The right buttock line is given a _____ value from zero.

24. The left buttock line is given a _____ value from zero.

25. Wing stations indicate positions on the _____ only.

26. Once a hard copy of a microfiche image has been used, it should be _____ .

27. In the design and construction of complex items, _____ are the most accurate way to communicate the information.

28. A _____ is a copy of the original working drawing for an aircraft part or group of parts, or for a design of a system or group of systems.

29. The three classes of working drawings are _____ , _____ , and _____ drawings.

30. The type of drawing that shows the relationship of parts and can be helpful in assembling components is called the _____ .

31. Wire sizes are frequently shown on the _____ diagram.

32. A _____ diagram shows pictorial sketches of the parts and the electrical connections between them.

33. A cabinet drawing is a type of _____ drawing.

34. Regardless of the number of views shown in a drawing, the _____ view is the principal one.

35. The _____ printed on the blueprint indicates the size of the part on the drawing as compared to the size of the actual part.

1. In engineering, which is referred to as the universal language?
   a. Drawings
   b. English
   c. Drafting
   d. Symbols

2. Which of these types of drawings is used to show internal detail more clearly than is possible in any other type of drawing?
   a. Sectional
   b. Assembly
   c. Installation
   d. Multi-detail

3. Which type of view indicates the object is viewed as if it were cut in half?
   a. Half-section
   b. Full-section
   c. Exploded
   d. Single-detail

4. The function of which of these types of drawings is to show an item in its completed shape?
   a. Assembly
   b. Installation
   c. Single-detail
   d. Full-section

5. Which of these types of drawings gives the information regarding mounting directions, location and dimensions, and attaching hardware?
   a. Assembly
   b. Installation
   c. Single-detail
   d. Block diagram

6. Which of these electrical wiring diagrams shows only external connections between units?
   a. Single-line
   b. Connection
   c. Interconnect
   d. Elementary

7. Which of these electrical wiring diagrams shows the path of an electrical circuit or system and components using graphic symbols?
   a. Single-line
   b. Connection
   c. Interconnect
   d. Elementary

8. Which of these diagrams depicts the flow of fluids in a system?
   a. Single-line
   b. Interconnect
   c. Mechanical schematic
   d. Electrical elementary schematic

9. Which of these electrical wiring diagrams can help in troubleshooting a circuit?
   a. Single-line
   b. Interconnect
   c. Mechanical schematic
   d. Electrical elementary schematic

Chapter 9:

Blueprints and Drawings

MULTIPLE CHOICE
QUESTIONS

name:

date:

Chapter 9: *Blueprints and Drawings*

MULTIPLE CHOICE QUESTIONS

name:

date:

10. Drawings for objects of uniform thickness generally show how many views?
    a. One
    b. Two
    c. Three
    d. Four

11. Which type of drawing is the truest representation of an object?
    a. Orthographic
    b. Perspective
    c. Isometric
    d. Oblique

12. Which type of drawing is **NOT** used in the manufacture or repair of aircraft, but may be used effectively for technical illustrations?
    a. Orthographic
    b. Perspective
    c. Cavalier
    d. Cabinet

13. Which type of line indicates that a portion of the object is not shown on the drawing?
    a. Phantom lines
    b. Extension lines
    c. Hidden lines
    d. Break lines

14. Which type of line indicates the relative position of a missing part?
    a. Phantom lines
    b. Extension lines
    c. Hidden lines
    d. Break lines

15. The title block for a print is usually found in the:
    a. Upper right-hand corner
    b. Upper left-hand corner
    c. Lower right-hand corner
    d. Lower left-hand corner

16. Zone numbers on drawings are read:
    a. Right to left
    b. Left to right
    c. From the top down
    d. From the bottom up

17. A numbering system is used in the design and manufacture of aircraft in order to identify any given point within the aircraft to within:
    a. One cubic foot
    b. One linear foot
    c. One cubic inch
    d. One half linear inch

18. The reference datum line for fuselage stations is designated by the:
    a. Aircraft manufacturer
    b. FAA
    c. AMT
    d. Engineer

19. The only datum that is the same on all aircraft is the:
    a. Centerline of the aircraft
    b. Fuselage station
    c. Waterline station
    d. Wing station

20. Which of these is used to show specific relationships between three variables?
    a. Rectilinear graph
    b. Circular chart
    c. Nomograph
    d. Pie chart

21. Which of these shows a relationship between two variables, one shown as vertical and one as horizontal?
    a. Rectilinear graph
    b. Bar chart
    c. Nomograph
    d. Pie chart

22. The first commercial airplane that was designed and exclusively drawn on computer is the:
    a. Boeing 767
    b. Airbus 320
    c. Boeing 777
    d. Boeing 747

23. In sketching drawings, what type of strokes should the technician use with his pencil?
    a. Bold
    b. Short
    c. Long
    d. Circular

24. Sketching lines, circles and arcs that will intersect lines are best done with:
    a. Marking pencil
    b. Calligraphy pen
    c. Drawing tools
    d. Colored pencils

25. Which of these can be placed on paper as guides when drawing freehand lines?
    a. Dots
    b. Map tacks
    c. Dashes
    d. Ruler

26. One of the objects that traditionally takes up extraordinary amounts of space in the business of aircraft maintenance is:
    a. Tool cabinet
    b. Break room
    c. Paperwork
    d. Office

27. Using CAD instead of manual design saves:
    a. Extensive erasure
    b. Printing
    c. Microfilming
    d. CAM

28. Which of these two types of drawings are most similar in appearance?
    a. Assembly and exploded view
    b. Full-section and interconnect
    c. Block diagram and logic flow chart
    d. Single-line diagram and single-detail drawing

29. If a rear view of an object needs to be shown in the drawing, it is customarily placed:
    a. To the left of the left-hand view
    b. To the right of the right-hand view
    c. To the left of the bottom view
    d. To the right of the front view

Chapter 9:
Blueprints and Drawings

MULTIPLE CHOICE QUESTIONS

name:

date:

Chapter 9:
Blueprints and Drawings

MULTIPLE CHOICE QUESTIONS

name:

date:

30. Isometric drawings show only:
    a. Angles
    b. Height and width
    c. External features
    d. Objects in perspective

31. The most common number of views shown in a drawing is:
    a. One
    b. Two
    c. Neither A nor B
    d. Both A and B

Chapter 9:
Blueprints and
Drawings

**ANALYSIS
QUESTIONS**

name:

date:

1. You are removing the aft galley assembly from a Boeing 737 aircraft. The galley assembly weighs in excess of 375 pounds, and is so large that it is split horizontally for ease of removal and installation. What kind of drawing would assist you in understanding how the galley is dismantled for removal from the aircraft?

2. What kind of drawing would best illustrate a bearing installed in an electric motor?

3. What type of drawing would show the main crankshaft bearing journals as installed in the crankcase?

4. You are troubleshooting a communication radio that intermittently cuts out while receiving. What diagrams or charts would you use to help you find and correct the source of the problem?

5. Assume that in Question 4 your troubleshooting points to a bad comm transceiver. What type of chart would an avionics technician use to troubleshoot the transceiver at an internal component level?

6. Assume in Question 4 that you determined the source of the intermittent cut out was a loose wire at a connector plug. What diagram would you use to determine which pin in the connector to repair?

7. You are rigging the nose gear doors on a Boeing 727 aircraft. What type of chart would help you understand the mechanical function of the landing gear door sequencing operation?

8. You have installed a set of STC'd drag-reducing wingtips on a Cessna 172. Weight and balance have not changed. What sort of drawing might you want to include in block 8 of Form 337 that you complete for this mod?

9. You have installed an STC'd weather radar unit in the right wing leading edge of a Cessna 210 aircraft. The radar CPU is installed in the aircraft baggage compartment and a display has been mounted in the instrument panel. What are some of the drawings used in this installation?

10. In Question 9, what drawings (in addition to the STC) would you include in Form 337?

11. How many views, and what sort of station information, would you use to illustrate weight and balance data for the radar receiver/transmitter in Question 9?

12. You are looking at a blueprint for a Boeing 737 aircraft to determine the correct material and dimensions for a cargo compartment floor beam. Your employer operates 737-300s, -500s, -700s and -900s. What information on the blueprint will tell you that the data on the print are correct for the particular aircraft you are working on?

Chapter 9:
Blueprints and Drawings

13. When installing the replacement cargo compartment floor beam mentioned in Question 12, you see that the print requires you to drill holes 1/4 inch in diameter and ream to 0.2515 inch. What is the tolerance?

14. What types of lines would you expect to see to illustrate a hidden hole in a side view of a part, and the diameter of the hole?

15. What kinds of lines would you use to show a flap assembly first in the retracted position, then in the fully extended position, in the same illustration?

1. There three categories of problems concerning aircraft weight and balance: over maximum weight, too much weight forward, and _____ .

2. An aircraft with too much weight forward will have decreased _____ .

3. _____ weight and _____ are determined at the time of certification.

4. Used aircraft have a tendency to gain weight because of _____ in areas that cannot be easily cleaned.

5. Balance is affected by changes in _____ and_____ .

6. The empty weight and corresponding CG of a new aircraft are determined and computed by t he _____ .

7. The horizontal distance between an item and the datum is known as the _____ .

8. The datum is an imaginary _____ from which all horizontal measurements are taken for balance purposes.

9. The total allowable aircraft weight including the aircraft and all of its contents is known as the
.

10. The _____ of an aircraft actually includes all fixed-location operating equipment and full oil.

11. MAC refers to the _____ chord.

12. The moment is the product of a weight and its _____ .

13. A 50-pound weight located 10 inches forward of the datum has a moment of _____ .

14. The _____ is the moment reduced by 10,000, 1,000, or 100 for ease of calculation.

15. The _____ is the distance between the forward and rearward CG limits.

16. The standard weight for aviation gas is _____ and the standard weight for turbine fuel is _____ .

17. Standard weight for an adult passenger in the summer is _____ .

18. _____ includes the weight of extra items on the weighing platform that are not a part of the item being weighed.

19. An aircraft's wheels or jack pads can be considered _____ .

Chapter 10:
Aircraft Weight and Balance

FILL IN THE BLANK QUESTIONS

name:

date:

Chapter 10: *Aircraft Weight and Balance*

FILL IN THE BLANK QUESTIONS

name:

date:

20. The _____ is the maximum allowable weight of a loaded aircraft without fuel.

21. Useful load is determined by subtracting _____ from _____ .

22. Information on the weight and balance of a particular aircraft can be found in _____ , _____ , and manufacturer's maintenance manuals.

23. The sample type certificate data sheet on page 10-9 states that the fuel capacity of the aircraft is _____ .

24. _____ should be drained before weighing an aircraft.

25. Before draining _____ from an aircraft, check the Aircraft Specification to determine whether the tanks should be full or empty.

26. When weighing an airplane using the wheels as weighing points, _____ should be used to hold the aircraft.

27. The distance from the main weighing point to the _____ must be known to determine the CG.

28. The _____ CG range is usually associated with older light aircraft.

29. Ballast can be used to shift the _____ .

30. The CG is the distance of the exact point of balance of an aircraft from the reference _____ .

31. The formula WS/TW=CG/D is used to calculate how much weight _____ .

32. _____ is used to determine the most forward CG limit of an aircraft.

33. The maximum weight of an aircraft is determined by adding the _____ to the weights of the pilots, passengers, oil, fuel, and baggage.

34. A list of approved equipment usually includes the item's weight and _____ .

35. Many helicopters have a more _____ CG range than airplanes do.

36. In the portion of a Type Certificate Data Sheet found on page 10-19, the _____ is a plumb line from the right inside top of the baggage compartment.

37. A _____ is used to determine the loading limits for a light training aircraft.

38. Commuter aircraft loading is calculated through use of a _____ .

39. The amount of fuel burned accounts for the difference in an aircraft's _____ and _____ weights.

Chapter 10:
Aircraft Weight
and Balance

**FILL IN THE BLANK
QUESTIONS**

name:

date:

Chapter 10:
Aircraft Weight and Balance

FILL IN THE BLANK
QUESTIONS

name:

date:

1. An overloaded aircraft will require all of these except:
   a. More runway
   b. Decreased stall speed
   c. Lower climb angle and higher speed
   d. More engine power

2. If an aircraft has to much weight aft, which of the following is **NOT** a possible result:
   a. Stability is decreased
   b. Flying speed is decreased
   c. The aircraft will have a tendency to dive
   d. Stall characteristics occur more readily

3. Periodic reweighing is required of:
   a. All aircraft
   b. All air carrier and air taxi aircraft
   c. All corporate and general aviation aircraft
   d. All corporate and air taxi aircraft

4. The turning effect on a fulcrum is known as the:
   a. Minute
   b. Moment
   c. Manual
   d. Mean

5. The arm, in the context of weight and balance, is:
   a. The gross weight of an object
   b. The distance from a weight to the aircraft centerline
   c. The volume of an object to be weighed
   d. The distance from a weight to the fulcrum point

6. Weight and balances data can be obtained from:
   a. Aircraft specifications
   b. Aircraft flight manuals
   c. Aircraft operating limitations
   d. All of the above

7. The imaginary vertical plan from which all horizontal measurements are taken for balance purposes is called the:
   a. Diorama
   b. Date
   c. Datum
   d. Data

8. The reference datum is always:
   a. At the nose of the aircraft
   b. Chosen by the manufacturer
   c. Chosen by the FAA
   d. At the aircraft center of gravity

9. The point at which the nose-heavy and tail-heavy moments are exactly equal in magnitude is the:
   a. Lever dorm
   b. Ballast point
   c. Center of gravity
   d. Empty weight

10. EWCG is an abbreviation for:
    a. External wing consistency generator
    b. Extra-width composite gas
    c. Empty weight center of gravity
    d. Empty weight competitive gain

Chapter 10:
Aircraft Weight and Balance

MULTIPLE CHOICE
QUESTIONS

name:

date:

Chapter 10: *Aircraft Weight and Balance*

11. When an aircraft with full oil is weighed, the weight of the oil must be subtracted from the result in order to determine the:
    a. Basic weight
    b. Empty weight
    c. Gross weight
    d. Tare weight

12. Many transport aircraft have multiple maximum weights. Which of the following is **NOT** commonly used:
    a. Maximum landing weight
    b. Maximum ramp weight
    c. Maximum takeoff weight
    d. Maximum zero fuel weight

13. The MAC of a constant-chord wing is the same as the:
    a. Actual chord of the wing
    b. Airfoil line
    c. Twice the wingspan
    d. Percentage of the MAC of a tapered-wing aircraft

14. The leading edge of the mean aerodynamic chord is referred to as the:
    a. REMAC
    b. LEMAC
    c. TEMAC
    d. Big MAC

15. Minimum fuel, where weight and balance are concerned, refers to:
    a. Super unleaded
    b. The minimum amount of fuel required to fly the aircraft
    c. The amount of fuel that must be shown in the weight and balance report when the aircraft is loaded for an extreme-conditions check
    d. Half the maximum except takeoff horsepower

16. The minimum fuel load for a small aircraft with a reciprocating engine is based on:
    a. Wingspan
    b. Engine horsepower
    c. The datum minus the arm
    d. FAA standards

17. A 12-pound weight located 30 inches forward of the datum would have a moment of:
    a. 360 lb.-in.
    b. −360 lb.-in.
    c. 42 lb.
    d. 360 lb.

18. A 20-pound weight located 100 inches aft of the datum would have a moment of:
    a. 120 lb.^{2}
    b. −2,000 lb.-in.
    c. 80 lb.-in.
    d. 2,000 lb.-in.

19. A standard child passenger seated 40 inches aft of the datum would have a moment of:
    a. 3,200 lb.-in.
    b. −3,200 lb.-in.
    c. 40 lb-in.
    d. 80 lb.

20. Turbine fuel weighs:
    a. 6.7 lb/gal
    b. 7.6 lb/gal
    c. 5.7 lb/gal
    d. 7.5 lb/gal

21. A longitudinal location on an aircraft measured from the datum is called a:
    a. Buttline
    b. CG
    c. Stringer line
    d. Station

22. Useful load does **NOT** include:
    a. Fuel
    b. Passengers
    c. Crew
    d. Seats

23. When preparing to weigh an aircraft the following information must be obtained:
    a. Fuel capacity
    b. Datum location
    c. Maximum weight
    d. All of the above

24. The first step in preparing an aircraft for weighing is:
    a. Drain the fuel
    b. Clean the aircraft
    c. Strip the paint
    d. Remove the radius

25. An aircraft's fuel tanks are drained in preparation for weighing. Any fuel remaining is called:
    a. Full oil
    b. Full fuel
    c. Residual fuel
    d. Diesel fuel

26. Items that are **NOT** regularly carried in flight:
    a. Should be removed before weighing
    b. Should be included in empty weight calculations
    c. Should be cleaned and replace prior to weighing
    d. Kept in baggage compartments

27. When an aircraft is being weighed, it should be located:
    a. In a closed hangar
    b. On a level parking space
    c. With the brakes locked
    d. Pointed into the wind

28. The parking brake should never be used to hold an aircraft on the scales because:
    a. They may accidentally release
    b. Brake fluid will leak onto the scale
    c. Chocks are always readily available
    d. They may place a side load on the scales

29. Once scale weighs and measurements are obtained, the following may be computed:
    a. Aircraft empty weight and aircraft empty CG
    b. Aircraft tare weight and datum
    c. Aircraft zero fuel weight and useful load
    d. Aircraft empty cg and cruise fuel weight

30. The net weight is the gross weight minus:
    a. MAC
    b. CG
    c. Tare weight
    d. Mean weight

Chapter 10:
Aircraft Weight and Balance

MULTIPLE CHOICE QUESTIONS

name:

date:

Chapter 10:
Aircraft Weight and Balance

31. When the CG location will cause problems with normal loading of an aircraft, what is generally used to correct the problem?
    a. Permanent ballast
    b. Temporary ballast
    c. Load shifting
    d. This problem cannot be corrected

MULTIPLE CHOICE QUESTIONS

name:

32. The CG changes when weight within the aircraft is shifted based on:
    a. The empty weight and the MAC
    b. The amount of weight and the distance it is moved
    c. Manufacturer's specifications
    d. The net weight divided by the station measurement

date:

33. The CG range of a typical helicopter, compared to that of a typical airplane, is:
    a. Much wider
    b. About half
    c. Much more restricted
    d. Based on atmospheric conditions

34. Which of these combinations of loaded airplane weight and loaded airplane moment would be outside of the CG moment envelope shown in Figure 10-5-2 shown below?
    a. 1,400 pounds, 50 lb-in. moment
    b. 1,200 pounds, 40 lb.-in. moment
    c. 1,600 pounds, 55 lb.-in. moment
    d. 1,400 pounds, 40 lb.-in. moment

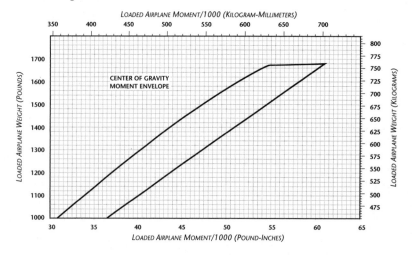

35. According to the fuel loading table (Table 10-5-5), the CG in inches of 35 gallons of fuel is:
    a. 261.4
    b. 261.6
    c. 261.8
    d. 262.1

FUEL LOADING TABLE JETA 6.8 LB/U.S. GALLONS			
GAL.	WT. (LBS.) 6.8 LBS/GAL	CG (IN.)	MOMENT (IN-LBS)
5	34.0	257.0	8738
10	68.0	258.7	17592
15	102.0	259.7	26489
20	136.0	260.5	35428
25	170.0	260.9	44353
30	204.0	261.2	53285
35	238.0	261.4	62213
40	272.0	261.6	71155
45	306.0	261.6	80050
50	340.0	261.7	88978
55	374.0	261.9	97951
60	408.0	262.1	106937
65	442.0	262.3	115937
70	476.0	262.6	124998
75	510.0	262.9	134079
80	544.0	263.0	143072
85	578.0	263.2	152130
90	612.0	263.4	161201

Chapter 10:
Aircraft Weight
and Balance

ANALYSIS
QUESTIONS

name:

date:

1. Explain why aircraft weight and balance are critical.

2. Why would someone need to reweigh an aircraft?

3. What is the datum of an aircraft? How is it used?

4. What is the difference between empty and basic weight?

5. Calculate the moment of a 10-pound seat placed at station 50.0.

6. What does it mean when the moment is a negative number?

7. Define the center of gravity (CG) of an aircraft. From what point is it measured?

8. What is the definition of the maximum weight of an aircraft? Is it always the same?

9. What does the term "minimum fuel" mean in relation to aircraft weight and balance?

10. What is the operating CG range? In what two ways can it be expressed?

11. What data crucial to weight and balance can be found on aircraft specifications and type certificate data sheets?

12. Describe briefly the steps in preparing an aircraft for weighing.

13. What measurements should you record when weighing an aircraft?

14. In order to shift an aircraft's center of gravity 5 inches forward, you need to move two standard adult passengers a certain distance. The total weight of the aircraft is 1,000 pounds. It is June 24. How far must the passengers be moved, and in which direction?

15. What adverse conditions might an overloaded or badly balanced helicopter encounter?

Chapter 10:
Aircraft Weight and Balance

ANALYSIS
QUESTIONS

name:

date:

1. It is _____ responsibility to maintain an aircraft in an airworthy condition.

2. Regulations governing all aspects of aeronautics are found in _____ .

3. If you discover unusual defects or repetitive problems while inspecting aircraft, the FAA encourages you to fill out and submit _____ .

4. To determine which records are permanent and must be retained by the aircraft owner, the best place to look would be _____ .

5. Engine operating parameters and minimum fuel grade suitable for use in the engine would be found in _____ .

6. _____ describes the regulations regarding the scope, procedures and recording of maintenance performed on type certificated aircraft.

7. _____ provides nonregulatory guidance on the preparation of aircraft maintenance records.

8. For specific type certificate information on rare or antique aircraft, propellers or engines you should look in _____ section of the Type Certificates.

9. _____ are the primary tool used by the FAA to inform aircraft owners and operators of conditions of an emergency nature.

10. Temporary records must be retained until the work performed is repeated or superceded by other work, or for _____ .

11. For information on the form and content of maintenance logbook entries, you should look in _ .

12. _____ are temporary regulations used to address an emergency issue that requires longer term study.

13. The Air Transport Association of America (ATA) issues specifications for manufacturer's technical data in _____ .

14. When you perform a major repair on an aircraft, you must complete _____ .

15. _____ are issued for restricted, limited and provisional category aircraft, and are effective for a limited period of time.

16. Airworthiness Directives are issued _____ .

Chapter 11:

Maintenance Documentation

FILL IN THE BLANK QUESTIONS

name:

date:

Chapter 11:
Maintenance
Documentation

FILL IN THE BLANK QUESTIONS

name:

date:

17. As their name implies, Advisory Circulars are basically informational in nature, not regulatory. An exception to this rule would be Advisory Circular _____ .

18. Advisory Circular _____ provides guidance on Airworthiness Directives.

19. The first two digits of an Airworthiness Directive designate _____ .

20. FAR _____ covers Agricultural Aircraft Operators.

21. Means for leveling an aircraft can be found in the aircraft's _____ .

22. To find the technical standards an aircraft must meet, you should look in _____ .

23. After completing a Form 337, you must deliver a copy to the aircraft owner and forward another copy to _____ .

24. When performing an annual or 100 hour inspection, you can use a checklist provided by the aircraft manufacturer or _____ .

25. When an aircraft is sold, its permanent records must _____ .

26. Keeping and maintaining an aircraft's maintenance records is the responsibility of _____ .

27. An aircraft received an annual inspection but was not found airworthy. The mechanic entering the inspection in the aircraft's log book must provide the aircraft owner with _____ .

28. Separate log books must be maintained for propellers, engines and _____ .

29. When you sign off an inspection, you must sign the log book and include _____ .

30. The standards that determine the way your AMT school operates can be found in _____ .

31. _____ must provide all the manuals necessary to service, operate, maintain and repair each product that they manufacture.

1. Which of the following is **NOT** required to be entered in the permanent aircraft records:
   a. Total time in service of the airframe
   b. Current status of applicable Airworthiness Directives
   c. Amount of oil added to the engine
   d. Current inspection status of the aircraft

2. To find information on your rights, privileges and limitations as a certificated mechanic, you should refer to:
   a. FAR Part 91
   b. AC 65-2a
   c. FAR Part 43
   d. FAR Part 65

3. You are performing a weight and balance check on an aircraft after a major repair. To find the aircraft's center of gravity range, you should look in:
   a. The aircraft logbook
   b. The applicable Type Certificate Data Sheet
   c. FAR Part 23, Airworthiness Standards
   d. The aircraft temporary records

4. You have completed a major alteration on a customer's aircraft. What should you do with copies of Form 337?
   a. Retain one for your files
   b. Deliver one to the aircraft owner for his records
   c. Submit one to the FAA within 48 hours
   d. All of the above

5. As part of an annual inspection, you should check on the status of pertinent Airworthiness Directives for the aircraft you are inspecting. You should look in:
   a. The AD Listings
   b. AC 39-7, Airworthiness Directives
   c. FAR Part 39, Airworthiness Directives
   d. None of the above

6. Compliance with Airworthiness Directives:
   a. Is at the discretion of the aircraft owner
   b. Is mandatory
   c. Can be postponed if the aircraft owner can't afford it
   d. Is determined by the aircraft manufacturer

7. A customer brings you a rare antique aircraft for an inspection. The best source of information on this aircraft would be:
   a. Trade-A-Plane
   b. Volume VI, Aircraft Listings
   c. Civil Air Regulations (CAR) Part 03
   d. FAR Part 43-13

8. When performing an annual inspection, you must use a checklist that at a minimum covers the items specified in:
   a. AC 43.13 appendix G
   b. AC 43.9
   c. FAR Part 91
   d. None of the above

9. When returning an aircraft to service after an inspection, which item is NOT required to be entered in the permanent records:
   a. A list of all parts and consumable items used in the inspection
   b. The type of inspection and a brief description of the extent of the inspection
   c. The signature, certificate number, and certificate type of the person approving or disapproving the aircraft for return to service
   d. The date of the inspection and aircraft total time in service

Chapter 11:

Maintenance Documentation

MULTIPLE CHOICE
QUESTIONS

name:

date:

Chapter 11:

Maintenance Documentation

MULTIPLE CHOICE
QUESTIONS

name:

date:

10. Temporary records:
    a. Can be kept or discarded at the aircraft owner's discretion
    b. Must be retained until the work is repeated or superceded by other work
    c. Must be retained and transferred when the aircraft is sold
    d. Can be discarded

11. Filling out an FAA Form 8010-4 Malfunction or Defect Report is:
    a. Mandatory
    b. Specified by the scope and detail section of FAR Part 43 appendix d
    c. Voluntary, and important to the continued safe operation of general aviation aircraft
    d. At the discretion of the aircraft owner

12. Digital manuals and computer maintenance aids:
    a. Are becoming more common in aviation maintenance
    b. Are replacing paper in all facets of aviation maintenance
    c. Demand computer literacy from aircraft maintenance technicians
    d. All of the above

13. Advisory Circular AC 43.13-1B Change 1 differs from other Advisory Circulars because:
    a. It contains FAA – approved data that can be referenced when performing repairs
    b. It is kept in a different book
    c. It is advisory in nature
    d. It is non-mandatory

14. A large air carrier is certificated under which part of the FARs?
    a. Part 127
    b. Part 91
    c. Part 145
    d. Part 121

15. When an aircraft owner presents evidence that his aircraft conforms to its type certificate, and any Supplemental Type Certificates and Airworthiness Directives, the FAA will grant him:
    a. Form 8050-1, Aircraft Registration
    b. Form 8100-2, Standard Aircraft Airworthiness Certificate
    c. Form 8120-4, Production Certificate
    d. Form 8110-2, Supplemental Type Certificate

16. FAA Form 8130-7, Special Airworthiness Certificate, is effective:
    a. Only on experimental aircraft
    b. Only on agricultural aircraft
    c. For a limited period of time
    d. Only on limited category aircraft

17. Which item listed below is NOT included in the maintenance record entry for an aircraft that has received an annual inspection and has been returned to service?
    a. A list of discrepancies and unairworthy items
    b. The type of inspection and a brief description of its extent
    c. The date of the inspection and aircraft total time in service
    d. The signature of the person returning the aircraft to service

18. Under some circumstances, such as private owners operating personal aircraft, temporary records are entered in the aircraft, powerplant or propeller log books. Which statement is most correct about these temporary records?
    a. They must be retained until the work is repeated or superceded
    b. They must include references to acceptable data
    c. Removal of these temporary records from the log books is inadvisable
    d. All of the above

19. Who is responsible for complying with an Airworthiness Directive?
    a. The aircraft owner
    b. The aircraft operator
    c. The aircraft lessor
    d. None of the above

20. Compliance with an Airworthiness Directive may be:
    a. One-time
    b. Recurrent
    c. Before further flight
    d. All of the above

21. Specific information on the regulations governing Identification and Registration marks can be found in:
    a. AC 45-2
    b. AC 43-13
    c. FAR Part 45
    d. None of the above

22. Information on methods of repair of acrobatic aircraft might be found in:
    a. FAR Part 43
    b. FAR Part 23
    c. AC 43.13
    d. AC 23-13

23. When filling out form 337 block 8, a description of the work performed, you must include:
    a. A checklist of your own design that conforms to appendix D of FAR Part 43
    b. Technical data acceptable to the Administrator of the FAA
    c. Standard industry practices.
    d. None of the above

24. Which form **MUST** an aircraft owner possess in order to operate his aircraft?
    a. FCC Radio Station License
    b. Certificate of Sanitary Construction
    c. Form 8050-2, Aircraft Registration
    d. State sales/use tax receipt

25. When providing a description of the work performed in Block 8 of Form 337, what is the correct method of completing the entry?
    a. Sign, date, and enter your certificate type and number
    b. Draw a line after your last entry and print the word "End"
    c. Entering the description is sufficient. Go on to Block 9
    d. None of the above

26. Which discrepancies discovered on an inspection do **NOT** have to be cleared before the aircraft can be returned to service?
    a. All discrepancies discovered on an inspection must be cleared prior to release
    b. The aircraft owner decides which discrepancies must be repaired prior to release of the aircraft
    c. FAR 43 Appendix D specifies those items not required for release
    d. You may placard items permitted to be inoperative under FAR Part 91.213(d)(2), mark the items "inoperative", and provide the owner a dated list of discrepancies

27. You must fill out a Form 337:
    a. When the aircraft is sold
    b. When you perform a major alteration or repair
    c. Upon completion of a progressive inspection
    d. When you apply for a Standard Airworthiness Certificate

28. How long must temporary records be retained for an executive or corporate aircraft?
    a. Until the aircraft is sold
    b. For a period of one year
    c. Until the work is repeated or supeceded, or after one year
    d. At the aircraft owner's discretion

Chapter 11:
Maintenance Documentation

MULTIPLE CHOICE QUESTIONS

name:

date:

Chapter 11:
Maintenance Documentation

MULTIPLE CHOICE
QUESTIONS

name:

date:

Refer to a copy of the TCDS for the Airbus A318 aircraft to answer the next five questions:

Chapter 11:
Maintenance Documentation

1. The maximum continuous thrust for a CFM56-5B9/P engine is _____ at an elevation of _____ and an ambient temperature of _____ .

2. The maximum takeoff weight for an 004 variant aircraft is _____ .

ANALYSIS
QUESTIONS

name:

3. The U.S.A. fuel grades approved for use in the A318-111 aircraft are mil spec _____ , and the American Society for Testing and Materials spec approved fuel grades are _____ .

date:

4. The number of this TCDS is _____ and it is on its _____ revision.

5. There are _____ total gallons of unusable fuel on a three-tank A318 aircraft.

6. You are performing an annual inspection on a Cessna 152 aircraft. What FAA publications would you consult in the course of your inspection?

7. Referring to Question 6, what manufacturer's manuals or publications would you consult in the course of your inspection?

8. Assume you are opening your own maintenance shop. What sort of information tools would you want to have in your shop?

9. When performing an annual inspection on a basic aircraft, what forms and document must be present for the inspection?

10. Assume you are performing an annual inspection on a Beechcraft Bonanza aircraft. Can you use any manual for this make and model aircraft?

Chapter 11:
Maintenance Documentation

**ANALYSIS
QUESTIONS**

name:

date:

1. The Federal Aviation Act of 1958 replaced _____ with the Federal Aviation Agency.

2. _____ gave the federal government the responsibility for air commerce and the enforcement of air safety rules.

3. Each component and system on an aircraft must meet the standards prescribed by _____ .

4. FAR Part 91, General Operating Rules, states no one may operate an aircraft unless it has had an inspection within _____ .

5. _____ may perform a 100-hour inspection on a general aviation aircraft used for hire and return the aircraft to service.

6. _____ may perform an annual inspection on a general aviation aircraft and return it to service.

7. The person most responsible for your health, safety and welfare on the job is _____ .

8. Studies show that that the proportion of all accidents caused by human error, not including design errors, is in the range of _____ percent.

9. The study of human body dimensions is known as _____ .

10. The science of _____ addresses issues of movement, leverage and strength.

11. _____ tasks involve a human monitoring a visual or auditory display for a particular event.

12. Team skills and coordination are a vital part of the _____ concept.

13. A team works together to accomplish _____ .

14. _____ is defined as a team situation in which members depend on one another to finish the final job.

15. For both airframe and powerplant ratings, a total of _____ documented experience performing the duties of both ratings must be submitted.

16. The minimum levels of stimuli needed for detection by each of our senses are called

_____ .

17. When a constant stimulus, whether physical or psychological, becomes imperceptible and we have adapted to dangerous or noxious environments, _____ occurs.

Chapter 12:
Privileges and Responsibilities

18. An FAA researcher has noted "the more we looked at problems in maintenance operations, particularly those of aging aircraft, the more we saw _____ as some part of the problem."

19. An emergency locater transmitter (ELT) is normally checked by_____ .

20. Flight through severe turbulence can cause _____ .

21. A change to an aircraft structure which causes it to deviate from its original type certificate is likely a _____ .

22. A good source for guidance on determining if a repair is a major repair is

    _____ .

23. _____ divide the required items of an annual inspection into shorter segments that are performed throughout the year, to keep the aircraft from being grounded for long periods of time.

24. _____ may involve the strengthening, reinforcing, or splicing of primary structural members or their replacement by riveting or welding.

25. Large aircraft (gross takeoff weight 12,500 pounds or more) must be inspected in accordance with a _____ .

26. ATC transponders must be checked every _____ .

27. To obtain an Inspection Authorization rating, an A&P technician must have been actively engaged in maintaining civil aircraft for at least _____ prior to applying for the IA exam.

28. A technician must have held both the airframe and powerplant ratings for a period of at least _____ prior to applying for an Inspection Authorization rating exam.

29. _____ may be issued to unlicensed personnel performing maintenance, inspection, manufacturing or alterations in FAA-approved repair stations.

30. A candidate for a repairman's certificate must have at least _____ experience in the practices and methods for which the person is to be employed.

31. A repairman's certificate is valid only as long as the technician is employed

    _____ .

32. To keep an A&P rating current, a technician must have worked for at least _____ performing the duties of a technician.

Chapter 12:
Privileges and
Responsibilities

MULTIPLE CHOICE
QUESTIONS

name:

date:

1. What type of inspection is normally performed by a pilot?
    a. Preflight inspection
    b. ELT function check
    c. Neither A nor B
    d. Both A and B

2. Preventive maintenance tasks such as changing engine oil or putting air in the tires must be performed by:
    a. An A&P technician
    b. The aircraft's owner if he holds a pilot license
    c. An A&P technician holding an IA rating
    d. Any of the above can perform preventive maintenance

3. Which of the following is **NOT** a requirement to obtain an A&P license?
    a. U.S. citizenship
    b. The ability to read, write, speak and understand the English language
    c. Being at least 18 years of age
    d. Satisfy training or experience requirements

4. To pass the General, Airframe or Powerplant written exam you must score at least:
    a. 60%
    b. 70%
    c. 75%
    d. 80%

5. Which of the following is **NOT** true about the persons portrayed on the newly designed A&P certificate?
    a. One of the persons is Wilbur Wright
    b. One of the persons is Orville Wright
    c. They are pilots
    d. They are mechanics

6. Which of the following persons can perform minor repairs of discrepancies discovered on an annual inspection?
    a. A technician holding an A&P license
    b. A person holding a repairman's certificate and qualified to perform the repairs
    c. A technician holding an A&P license with IA rating
    d. All of the above

7. Which of the following persons can return an aircraft to service following an annual inspection?
    a. A technician holding an A&P license
    b. A person holding a repairman's certificate and qualified to perform the repairs
    c. A technician holding an A&P license with IA rating
    d. All of the above

8. Which of the following could be described as an "on condition" inspection as opposed to a "time controlled" inspection?
    a. Overweight or hard landing inspection
    b. Altimeter/static system check
    c. Transponder check
    d. ELT check

9. Studies have shown that human error is a factor in what percentage of all accidents?
    a. 33%
    b. 50%
    c. 60-80%
    d. 90%

Chapter 12:
Privileges and Responsibilities

10. Which of the following is **NOT** a characteristic of an effective team?
    a. Clear purpose
    b. Information hoarding
    c. Disagreement
    d. Shared leadership

11. Studies have shown that an effective team should not exceed:
    a. Eight members
    b. Nine members
    c. Ten members
    d. Twelve members

12. Which of the following would qualify as a major repair?
    a. Replacing an aircraft engine
    b. Replacing an aircraft propeller
    c. Replacing aircraft skin and stringers damaged by a ground vehicle
    d. Replacing a navigation light lamp

13. Select the statement that is most correct regarding human factors training.
    a. A. It is required by regulation
    b. Gains in productivity and safety outweigh training costs
    c. Studies show that human factors training has little impact on safety
    d. Is a waste of time

14. As an Airframe and Powerplant mechanic, you may **NOT** make any repair to:
    a. Engines
    b. Propellers
    c. Instruments
    d. Defects found during an annual inspection

15. Which of the following personnel can return an aircraft to service after a 100-hour inspection?
    a. A technician holding an A&P license
    b. The aircraft owner if he or she holds a pilot license
    c. A certificated repairman
    d. None of the above

16. For information regarding the requirements for an aircraft mechanic license, you should look in:
    a. AC65-19A
    b. FAR 61 appendix D
    c. AC43-13-1B
    d. FAR Part 65 Subpart D

17. Which statement regarding continuous inspection programs is most correct?
    a. You must use a current inspection program recommended by the FAA.
    b. You can use any inspection program established by the registered owner or operator and approved by the FAA.
    c. You must use an approved aircraft inspection program approved under FAR Section 125.419.
    d. You can use any continuous airworthiness inspection program of your choice as long as it meets the requirements of AC43 Appendix D.

18. A task that requires constant monitoring of a process or repetitive performance of a process is called a:
    a. Routine task
    b. Habituation task
    c. Vigilance task
    d. Stereotype task

19. Stress can be caused by:
    a. Working at night
    b. Time pressure
    c. Poor facilities
    d. All of the above

20. One result of excessive workload can be:
    a. Failure to identify a problem
    b. Maintaining a high standard of quality
    c. Improving your capacity for more work
    d. A feeling of pride and accomplishment

21. On a hard landing inspection you would look for:
    a. Worn tires
    b. Pulled rivets
    c. Signs of corrosion
    d. Lightning strike pinholes

22. As a maintenance technician, you would most likely inspect an emergency locator transmitter for:
    a. Operation
    b. Evidence of an operational check within the preceding 24 months
    c. The battery replacement date
    d. Presence of a tamper resistant seal

23. Which of the following items is a major repair:
    a. Replacing an engine with a serviceable one of the same model
    b. Replacing a landing gear trunnion by welding it in place
    c. Replacing a propeller with a serviceable one of the same type
    d. All of the above

24. An aircraft owner/pilot goes pleasure flying with friends and splits the cost of fuel. Aircraft used in this manner require:
    a. An annual inspection
    b. A 100-hour inspection
    c. A progressive inspection
    d. A continuous inspection program designed by the aircraft manufacturer

25. An owner/pilot uses her aircraft for flight instruction. The aircraft will need:
    a. An annual inspection
    b. A 100-hour inspection
    c. A progressive inspection
    d. A mode C transponder inspection

26. A progressive inspection:
    a. Covers the scope and detail of an annual inspection, but is broken into smaller segments
    b. Is the same as an annual inspection
    c. Is the same as a 100-hour inspection
    d. Is performed on aircraft of 12,500 pounds gross weight or greater

27. FAR 43.9 states that each person that maintains, rebuilds or alters an aircraft must:
    a. Use a checklist that conforms to AC 43 Appendix D
    b. Fill out a form 337
    c. Make a maintenance entry in the equipment's maintenance record
    d. Be appropriately rated in accordance with FAR Part 65

Chapter 12:
Privileges and Responsibilities

MULTIPLE CHOICE QUESTIONS

name:

date:

Chapter 12:
Privileges and Responsibilities

MULTIPLE CHOICE QUESTIONS

name:

date:

28. After performing a hazardous task hundreds of times without being injured, we become used to the danger and tend to ignore potentially dangerous indicators. This is called:
    a. A vigilance task
    b. Familiarity
    c. Competence
    d. Habituation

29. The purpose of studying human factors is:
    a. Saving your employer money
    b. Complying with regulations
    c. Reducing human errors that compromise public safety
    d. There is little value in studying human factors

30. In order to perform a 100-hour inspection, an A&P technician must:
    a. Have performed the work before
    b. Obtain an Inspection Authorization rating
    c. Have worked at least six months
    d. Do nothing. Having the A&P license is sufficient

1. You replace the engine on a Beechcraft Bonanza with a new engine of the same type. Why is this considered a minor repair?

2. A customer owns an executive jet and wants you to replace the cloth passenger seat covers with leather seat covers. The leather seat covers weigh the same as the cloth covers. What kind of alteration is this?

3. An aircraft's strobe lights fail to operate. You troubleshoot the problem and determine the strobe power supply is defective, and replace it with a serviceable part with the same part number. What kind of alteration/repair is this?

4. In Question 3, what action is required to return the aircraft to service, and who can do this?

5. A customer has you install a strobe light system on his aircraft, which did not previously have one. What kind of alteration/repair is this? What further maintenance action is required?

6. For the example in Question 5, what paperwork will you need to complete?

7. For the example in Question 5, what licenses/ratings would you need to possess to inspect the repair and return the aircraft to service?

8. You are performing an annual inspection on a customer's aircraft. The aircraft owner is present, and has told you he wants the inspection finished quickly. Your last checklist item requires you to remove a panel and check for corrosion and obvious damage. You have done the same task to the same type of aircraft, and you have never discovered corrosion or damage. You consider signing the item without performing the task. What human factors considerations are at work here?

9. While working a sheetmetal repair on a Boeing 757 door frame, you notice a fellow team member about to begin grinding corrosion on a floor beam without wearing eye protection. What would you do? What characteristics of effective teamwork are displayed in this scenario?

10. A large corporation owns a Boeing 737 that they use for executive transport. They hire you to develop an inspection program for the aircraft. The continuous airworthiness inspection programs for aircraft operated under Parts 121, 127 and 135 do not apply to your client's aircraft, in part because it has a low utilization rate. What are your options?

11. The floor panels in Boeing aircraft are simple honeycomb composite panels that bear no structural aircraft loads. On the other hand, the floor panels in Airbus A320 Series aircraft are load-bearing structural members that require complex and precise repair procedures. What human factors characteristic(s) might cause a technician to apply a Boeing repair on an Airbus floor panel?

Chapter 12:
Privileges and Responsibilities

ANALYSIS
QUESTIONS

name:

date:

Chapter 12:
Privileges and Responsibilities

ANALYSIS QUESTIONS

name:

date:

12. Assume you are a technician working night shift at a Part 121 air carrier. It is 2 hours until your aircraft is scheduled to depart, you have 2 inspection task cards to complete and feel this is not sufficient time. What human factors issues are apparent here?

13. What aspects of effective teamwork would help resolve the issues raised in Question 12?

14. You hold an A&P license with an IA rating. You have performed an annual inspection on a customer's aircraft and listed the unairworthy items, all of which are minor repairs. The aircraft owner/pilot wants to perform the work to correct the unairworthy items, which are not preventive maintenance items. Can he do this, and who is responsible for his work?

1. Public outcry over the death of _____ in 1931 led to the formation of the Civil Aeronautics Agency.

2. The CAA was instrumental in developing regulations that required periodic

   _____

3. Two of the reasons aircraft inspections are done are _____ .

4. In order to suit the inspection program to the aircraft, FARs set inspection requirements based on aircraft _____ .

5. According to FAR 91.409, aircraft with gross takeoff weights of _____ or less are basic aircraft.

6. An annual inspection can be performed only by an airframe and powerplant mechanic holding an _____ rating.

7. Basic aircraft must have an inspection performed once every _____ months.

8. A checklist that describes minimum inspection items is found in _____.

9. Continuous inspection programs were developed for complex aircraft to maintain _____ while minimizing _____ .

10. MSG-1 stands for _____ and was formed to address the complexity of the new _____ .

11. The first primary maintenance process was called _____ .

12. The second primary maintenance process, developed by MSG-1, was called _____.

13. _____ monitor a component's mechanical performance to keep failure rates below a certain threshold.

14. Monitoring and analyzing mechanical performance without mandatory inspection or servicing is called _____ .

15. The most basic tools you will use to inspect aircraft are your _____ .

16. _____ is the most common and most cost-effective inspection method.

17. One of the most commonly used precision measuring tools is the _____ which can measure length, width and thickness.

18. Ultrasonic and radiographic testing are two types of _____ .

Chapter 13:
Aircraft
Inspection

FILL IN THE BLANK QUESTIONS

name:

date:

Chapter 13:
Aircraft Inspection

FILL IN THE BLANK QUESTIONS

name:

date:

19. The two types of penetrant material are _____ .

20. The first step in dye penetrant inspection is _____ .

21. _____ are used to dissolve grease, sealants, wax and paint.

22. Molten salt baths cannot be used to clean _____ .

23. Corrosion and rust are removed with _____ .

24. Penetrant can be applied only after the part is thoroughly _____ .

25. Excess penetrant can cause _____ .

26. Developer dwell time is _____ the penetrant dwell time.

27. A disadvantage to ultrasonic inspection is that it is subject to _____ where it cannot detect flaws.

28. Ultrasonic units detect _____ signals and change them into _____ signals.

29. Ultrasonic inspection measures the changes in _____ of the sound waves as they pass through a material.

30. Longitudinal waves are used in the _____ method, generally on objects 1/2 inch or thicker.

31. Transverse waves are used in the _____ method which allows inspection of irregularly shaped components.

32. The two ways to perform ultrasonic inspections are the _____ and _____ .

33. Delamination and debonding in aircraft structures can be detected by _____ .

34. _____ detects sounds made by structures under conditions of stress.

35. _____ detects the relative amounts of heat in components to find cracks and corrosion.

36. A component being tested using eddy current inspection must be an _____ .

37. Eddy currents are induced in a conductor by a _____ .

38. Radiographic inspection uses _____ and _____ to detect flaws in aircraft structures and components.

39. The most distinguishing characteristic of x-rays is their _____ .

40. Iridium-192 is a type of _____ used to produce gamma rays for aircraft inspections.

41. The _____ of the material to be tested determines the level of radiation energy to use.

42. The quality of the contrast in the final image can be reduced by _____ .

43. Scattered radiation exposing false images on the film is called _____ .

44. Scattering can be controlled by placing _____ in critical areas of the test piece.

45. _____ is the property of some materials that causes them to emit visible light when subjected to radiation.

46. CT is a radiation inspection that can provide _____ and _____ images of cross sections of a test component.

47. The three factors which determine your level of exposure to ionizing radiation are _____ , _____ and _____ .

48. Devices called _____ measure personnel exposure levels to ionizing radiation.

49. The ease with which a part can be magnetized is called its _____ .

50. The magnetic field should be at _____ angles to the suspected defect for best results.

51. Maximum magnetic field disruption is achieved with _____ and _____ .

52. _____ refers to a metal's tendency to keep a magnetic field after the magnetizing current is removed.

53. The two methods used to magnetize components in magnetic particle inspections are the _____ method and the _____ method.

Chapter 13:
Aircraft
Inspection

FILL IN THE BLANK QUESTIONS

name:

date:

Chapter 13: Aircraft Inspection

FILL IN THE BLANK QUESTIONS

name:

date:

54. At the completion of the magnetic particle inspection procedure _____ is performed to remove residual magnetism.

55. Pressurized pneumatic systems can be checked using a leak detection solution such as _____ .

56. Never allow any part of your body to get close to areas where _____ may have leakage while the system is operating.

57. Faulty aircraft wiring or insulation can lead to _____ , _____ , and _____ .

58. _____ allows a structure to retain its required residual strength for a period of time after the failure of a principle structural element.

59. _____ is frequently used on electrical system conducts because it is resistant to corrosion.

60. Two of the most corrosion-prone areas you will encounter on an aircraft are the _____ and the _____ .

Chapter 13:
Aircraft
Inspection

MULTIPLE CHOICE
QUESTIONS

name:

date:

1. Which of the following is NOT considered a basic aircraft?
   a. Reciprocating engine-powered aircraft
   b. Gross takeoff weight 12500 lbs or less
   c. Aircraft having more than one engine
   d. Single engine turbine-powered fixed-wing aircraft

2. Which of the following can perform an annual inspection on basic aircraft?
   a. A mechanic with an airframe certification
   b. A mechanic with a powerplant certification
   c. A mechanic with both certifications but not IA rated
   d. A certified repair station rated for the particular aircraft being inspected

3. Which of the following is **NOT** an option for a continuous inspection program for the owner or operator of a complex aircraft?
   a. A current program recommended by the aircraft manufacturer
   b. A program currently in use by a person holding an air carrier operating certificate issued under Part 121, 127, or 135
   c. A program the operator developed and had approved by the FAA
   d. A checklist from FAR 43 Appendix D

4. What type of interval inspection is done once a month or every 300-500 flight hours?
   a. D check
   b. C check
   c. B check
   d. A check

5. Which interval inspection involves gutting the aircraft and repairing all damaged structure?
   a. B check
   b. D check
   c. A check
   d. C check

6. Which Maintenance Steering Group Task Force applies to the Boeing 757 and the Airbus 320?
   a. MSG-1
   b. MSG-2
   c. MSG-3
   d. MSG-4

7. Which of the following is a scheduled task under MSG-3?
   a. Restoration (RS)
   b. Inspection/Functional Check (IN/FC)
   c. Lubrication/Servicing (LU/SV)
   d. All of the above

8. Which of the following is an unscheduled task under MSG-3?
   a. Discards (DS)
   b. Data analysis (reliability)
   c. Reports of malfunctions (pilot or maintenance reports)
   d. Both B and C

9. A vernier micrometer is accurate to:
   a. One-thousandth of an inch
   b. One inch
   c. One ten-thousandth of an inch
   d. One-tenth of an inch

10. Which of the following is an agent for cleaning before dye penetrant inspection?
    a. Detergents
    b. Acids
    c. Alkalis
    d. All of the above

Chapter 13:
Aircraft Inspection

MULTIPLE CHOICE QUESTIONS

name:

date:

11. Which of the following is **NOT** a method for applying a penetrant?
    a. Spraying
    b. Immersion
    c. Brushing
    d. Etching

12. Upon inspection, which of the following indications results from a porous condition of the metal?
    a. Continuous line
    b. Small dots
    c. Sponge-like surface
    d. None of the above

13. False indications can be caused by which of the following?
    a. Poor quality penetrant
    b. Poor technician eyesight
    c. Inadequate penetrant removal
    d. None of the above

14. Which of the following inspection methods does **NOT** use sound waves?
    a. Tap testing
    b. Eddy current inspection
    c. Ultrasonic Leak testing
    d. Acoustic emission testing

15. Radiographic inspection can cause which of the following?
    a. Genetic mutations
    b. Flaws in structures to turn green
    c. Flaws to show up as lighter images on the film
    d. None of the above

16. Gamma rays contain how many times the energy of visible light?
    a. 1000 times
    b. 100000 times
    c. 10000 times
    d. 10 times

17. Which of the following is a special radiographic technique used in aircraft inspection?
    a. Positron emission tomography
    b. Computed tomography
    c. Colonoscopy
    d. Absorption

18. One main advantage of fluoroscope inspection is:
    a. Provides an instantaneous visible image of a component's interior
    b. The technician has to ingest barium
    c. The internal structures are not hidden or shaded by other structures in the beam path
    d. The component must be small enough to fit inside the scanner

19. Radiation levels used in aviation are:
    a. Less than those used in medical applications
    b. About the same as those used in medical applications
    c. Much greater than those used in medical applications
    d. So low that you need not be concerned about your exposure

20. Magnetic Particle Inspection detects flaws in alloys composed of:
    a. Iron or steel
    b. Aluminum or brass
    c. Glass or plastic
    d. Teflon

21. The residual method of component magnetization has the advantage of:
    a. Being used to detect subsurface flaws
    b. Being used on parts with low retentivity
    c. Allowing parts to be magnetized and then inspected later
    d. A three-way magnetic field

22. One advantage of applying magnetic particles with the dry method is:
    a. It needs no special application equipment
    b. It must be mixed with an anticorrosion agent
    c. It can cover oddly shaped parts completely
    d. It does not require the technician to wear a wet suit

23. Flaked paint in or around a rivet indicates:
    a. The rivet is too tight
    b. The rivet is too loose
    c. A deformed shop head
    d. A deformed rivet

24. Aircraft hydraulic systems operate at pressures up to:
    a. 300 psi
    b. 3000 psi
    c. 30,000 psi
    d. 1000 psi

25. If grease is exposed to pure oxygen, it will:
    a. Melt
    b. Freeze
    c. Do nothing
    d. Ignite

26. When an oxygen generator is activated it:
    a. Leaks oxygen
    b. Emits a rotten egg smell
    c. Releases an inert gas
    d. Changes color

27. An oxygen generator has special handling requirements and regulations relating to shipment and disposal because it is classified as a/an:
    a. PSU
    b. Compressed gas
    c. Pyrotechnic device
    d. Percussion device

28. Damage tolerance based inspections are developed:
    a. Based on an engineering evaluation of likely sites where damage could occur
    b. After the damage has occurred
    c. By the technician
    d. Without considering stress levels, damage growth rates, or material characteristics

29. The single greatest threat to the integrity of airframe structures is:
    a. Accidental damage
    b. Fatigue damage
    c. Air speed
    d. Corrosion

30. Damage to aircraft wiring is frequently caused by:
    a. Technicians
    b. Weather
    c. Rotting floorboards
    d. None of the above

Chapter 13:
Aircraft
Inspection

MULTIPLE CHOICE
QUESTIONS

name:

date:

Chapter 13:

Aircraft Inspection

MULTIPLE CHOICE QUESTIONS

name:

date:

31. Which type of corrosion occurs most likely under polyurethane finishes?
    a. Filiform
    b. Galvanic
    c. Fretting
    d. Pitting

32. On painted surfaces, corrosion can:
    a. Change the color of the paint
    b. Cause a scaly or blistered surface
    c. Be disguised by more paint
    d. Both A and B

33. Which of these can act as a corrosive agent?
    a. Microorganisms
    b. Water
    c. Air pollution
    d. All of the above

34. A list of items that must be maintained and inspected per FAR 121.369 is called:
    a. Required inspection items
    b. Inspection maintenance manual
    c. Regulated inspection items
    d. Required inspection iterations

35. According to the FAA, who is responsible for determining the airworthiness of parts used?
    a. The pilot
    b. The technician who installs the parts
    c. The manufacturer of the part
    d. The FAA

36. What form should accompany all rotable airworthy components?
    a. The Airworthiness Approval Tag Form 8130-3
    b. The FAA Approved Parts List
    c. The manufacturer's warranty
    d. The Airworthiness Part Number

1. You are working on a QEC (quick engine change) build up on a spare CFM-56 engine. Three task blocks on the build up checklist call for installation of the integrated drive generator, installation of the engine mounts, and installation of the hydraulic pump. Which of these tasks is a required inspection item?

2. While performing an annual inspection on a Cessna 210, you discover that the alternator needs to be replaced. The aircraft owner brings you an alternator that he wants you to install on his aircraft. The alternator looks new, but lacks documentation. What should you do?

3. You need to inspect a turbine engine rotor shaft for defects. The engine is on the wing. Would you use ultrasonic or radiographic inspection, or both?

4. You need to inspect a landing gear strut for defects. Radiographic inspection could detect flaws inside this heavy casting. Is it advisable to use radiographic inspection in this instance?

5. You are assigned a task card requiring you to pack and install an escape slide/raft assembly on a passenger door. Is this an RII?

6. Which area would you expect to be most prone to corrosion – landing gear wells, structure below galley areas, passenger door interior components, or engine pylons?

7. As you know, there are many safety precautions you should observe any time you perform work on aircraft. What special precautions should you exercise when performing sheetmetal repairs in the vicinity of electrical wiring?

8. What is the single most important consideration when performing dye penetrant inspection?

9. You change main landing gear wheel assembly on an A319 aircraft. Is this an RII?

10. It is a common practice to ship fish by air. Boeing and Airbus maintenance documentation specify special inspections after spillage from a fish shipment. What do you think happens if this spillage is not cleaned and the structure treated?

11. What inspection techniques can be used on composite structures?

12. Describe a major difference between an annual inspection and a progressive inspection regarding licenses and ratings of personnel performing the inspection.

13. What do all mechanical and electronic inspection aids have in common?

Chapter 13: Aircraft Inspection

ANALYSIS
QUESTIONS

name:

date:

Chapter 13:
Aircraft
Inspection

ANALYSIS
QUESTIONS

name:

date:

14. A pilot report states an aircraft's propeller struck a large bird in flight. The engine manual calls for a crankshaft runout inspection. What inspection aid would you use?

15. Refer to Question 14. You suspect the bird impact may have cracked the propeller mounting flange on the crankshaft. What inspection method should be applied here?

16. From what you have read about various inspection aids, what do you feel is the most distinguishing feature of radiographic testing methods?

17. Aircraft manufacturers require periodic treatment of fuel tanks with bacterial killing compounds. Why is this done?

18. Is checking the contents of an onboard emergency medical kit an RII?

19. Which inspection method would be more effective to detect an impending bearing failure on an operating electric motor – ultrasonic leak detection or thermography?